THE SECRETS OF DR. TAVERNER

OTHER BOOKS BY DION FORTUNE:

The Demon Lover
The Winged Bull
The Goat Foot God
Moon Magic
The Sea Priestess

Esoteric Philosophy of Love and Marriage
Esoteric Orders and Their Work
The Training and Work of an Initiate
Sane Occultism
Psychic Self-Defence
Practical Occultism in Daily Life
The Mystical Qabalah
The Cosmic Doctrine
Through the Gates of Death

THE SECRETS
OF DR. TAVERNER

by Dion Fortune

ARIEL PRESS
Columbus, Ohio

8|00

This book is made possible by a gift
to the Publications Fund of Light
by Leslie Swanson

240 p.

THE SECRETS OF DR. TAVERNER

ISBN 0-89804-137-6

L

TABLE OF CONTENTS

Introduction

These stories may be looked at from two standpoints, and no doubt the standpoint the reader chooses will be dictated by personal taste and previous knowledge of the subject under discussion. They may be regarded as fiction, designed, like the conversation of the Fat Boy recorded in *The Pickwick Papers*, "to make your flesh creep," or they may be considered to be what they actually are, studies in little-known aspects of psychology put in the form of fiction because, if published as a serious contribution to science, they would have no chance of a hearing.

It may not unreasonably be asked what motive anyone could have for securing a hearing for such histories as are set forth in these tales, beyond the not unreasonable interest in the royalties that usually fall to the lot of those who cater for the popular taste in horrors; I would ask my readers, however, to credit me with another motive than the purely commercial. I was one of the earliest students of psychoanalysis in this country, and I found, in the course of my studies, that the ends of a number of threads were put into my hands, but that the threads disappeared into the darkness that surrounded the small circle of light thrown by exact scientific knowledge. It was in following these threads out into the darkness of the Unknown that I came upon the experiences and cases which, turned into fiction, are set down in these pages.

I do not wish to imply by that, however, that these stories all happened exactly as set down, for such is not the case; they are, however, all founded on fact, and there is not a single incident herein contained which is pure imagination. That is to say, while no picture is an actual photograph, not one is an imaginary sketch; they are rather composite photographs, obtained by cutting out and piecing together innumerable snapshots of actual happenings, and the whole, far from being an arbitrary product of the imagination, is a serious study in the psychology of ultra-consciousness.

I present these studies in super-normal pathology to the general reader because it has been my experience that such cases as I chronicle here are by no manner of means as uncommon as might be supposed, but, being unrecognized, pass unhelped. I have personally come across several instances of the Power House, some of which are well known to the members of the different coteries who are interested in these matters; "Blood-Lust" is literally true, and both these stories, far from being written up for the purposes of fiction, have been toned down to make them fit for print.

"Dr. Taverner" will no doubt be recognized by some of my readers; his mysterious nursing home was an actual fact, and infinitely stranger than any fiction could possibly be. It is a curious thing that the picture of him drawn from fancy by the artist who illustrated these stories for the *Royal Magazine* is a recognizable likeness, although that artist had neither seen a photograph nor had a description of him.

To "Dr. Taverner" I owe the greatest debt of my life; without "Dr. Taverner" there would have been no 'Dion Fortune,' and to him I offer the tribute of these pages.

—Dion Fortune, *London.*

THE SECRETS
OF DR. TAVERNER

BLOOD-LUST

I

I have never been able to make up my mind whether Dr. Taverner should be the hero or the villain of these histories. That he was a man of the most selfless ideals could not be questioned, but in his methods of putting these ideals into practice he was absolutely unscrupulous. He did not evade the law, he merely ignored it, and though the exquisite tenderness with which he handled his cases was an education in itself, yet he would use that wonderful psychological method of his to break a soul to pieces, going to work as quietly and methodically and benevolently as if bent upon the cure of his patient.

The manner of my meeting with this strange man was quite simple. After being gazetted out of the R.A.M.C. I went to a medical agency and inquired what posts were available.

I said: "I have come out of the Army with my nerves shattered. I want some quiet place till I can pull myself together."

"So does everybody else," said the clerk.

He looked at me thoughtfully. "I wonder whether you would care to try a place we have had on our books for some time. We have sent several men down to it but none of them would stop."

He sent me round to one of the tributaries of Harley Street, and there I made the acquaintance of the man who, whether he was good or bad, I have always regarded as the greatest mind I ever met.

Tall and thin, with a parchment-like countenance, he might have been any age from thirty-five to sixty-five. I

3

have seen him look both ages within the hour. He lost no time in coming to the point.

"I want a medical superintendent for my nursing home," he told me. "I understand that you have specialized, as far as the Army permitted you to, in mental cases. I am afraid you will find my methods very different from the orthodox ones. However, as I sometimes succeed where others fail, I consider I am justified in continuing to experiment, which I think, Dr. Rhodes, is all any of my colleagues can claim to do."

The man's cynical manner annoyed me, though I could not deny that mental treatment is not an exact science at the present moment. As if in answer to my thought he continued:

"My chief interest lies in those regions of psychology which orthodox science has not as yet ventured to explore. If you will work with me you will see some queer things, but all I ask of you is, that you should keep an open mind and a shut mouth."

This I undertook to do, for, although I shrank instinctively from the man, yet there was about him such a curious attraction, such a sense of power and adventurous research, that I determined at least to give him the benefit of the doubt and see what it might lead to. His extraordinarily stimulating personality, which seemed to key my brain to concert pitch, made me feel that he might be a good tonic for a man who had lost his grip on life for the time being.

"Unless you have elaborate packing to do," he said, "I can motor you down to my place. If you will walk over with me to the garage I will drive you round to your lodgings, pick up your things, and we shall get in before dark."

We drove at a pretty high speed down the Portsmouth road till we came to Thursley, and, then, to my surprise, my companion turned off to the right and took the big car by a cart track over the heather.

"This is Thor's Ley or field," he said, as the blighted

4

country unrolled before us. "The old worship is still kept up about here."

"The Catholic faith?" I inquired.

"The Catholic faith, my dear sir, is an innovation. I was referring to the pagan worship. The peasants about here still retain bits of the old ritual; they think that it brings them luck, or some such superstition. They have no knowledge of its inner meaning." He paused a moment, and then turned to me and said with extraordinary emphasis: "Have you ever thought what it would mean if a man who had the Knowledge could piece that ritual together?"

I admitted I had not. I was frankly out of my depth, but he had certainly brought me to the most unchristian spot I had ever been in my life.

His nursing home, however, was in delightful contrast to the wild and barren country that surrounded it. The garden was a mass of colour, and the house, old and rambling and covered with creepers, as charming within as without; it reminded me of the East, it reminded me of the Renaissance, and yet it had no style save that of warm rich colouring and comfort.

I soon settled down to my job, which I found exceedingly interesting. As I have already said, Taverner's work began where ordinary medicine ended, and I have under my care cases such as the ordinary doctor would have referred to the safe keeping of an asylum, as being nothing else but mad. Yet Taverner, by his peculiar methods of work, laid bare causes operating both within the soul and in the shadowy realm where the soul has its dwelling, that threw an entirely new light upon the problem, and often enabled him to rescue a man from the dark influences that were closing in upon him. The affair of the sheep-killing was an interesting example of his methods.

5

II

One showery afternoon at the nursing home we had a call from a neighbor—not a very common occurrence, for Taverner and his ways were regarded somewhat askance. Our visitor shed her dripping mackintosh, but declined to loosen the scarf which, warm as the day was, she had twisted tightly round her neck.

"I believe you specialize in mental cases," she said to my colleague. "I should very much like to talk over with you a matter that is troubling me."

Taverner nodded, his keen eyes watching her for symptoms.

"It concerns a friend of mine—in fact, I think I may call him my *fiance*, for, although he has asked me to release him from his engagement, I have refused to do so; not because I should wish to hold a man who no longer loved me, but because I am convinced that he still cares for me, and there is something which has come between us that he will not tell me of.

"I have begged him to be frank with me and let us share the trouble together, for the thing that seems an insuperable obstacle to him may not appear in that light to me; but you know what men are when they consider their honour is in question." She looked from one to the other of us smiling. No woman ever believes that her men folk are grown up; perhaps she is right. Then she leant forward and clasped her hands eagerly. "I believe I have found the key to the mystery. I want you to tell me whether it is possible or not."

"Will you give me particulars?" said Taverner.

"We got engaged while Donald was stationed here for his training (that would be nearly five years ago now), and there was always the most perfect harmony between us until he came out of the Army, when we all began to notice a change in him. He came to the house as often as ever, but he always seemed to want to avoid being alone with me.

6

We used to take long walks over the moors together, but he has absolutely refused to do this recently. Then, without any warning, he wrote and told me he could not marry me and did not wish to see me again, and he put a curious thing in his letter. He said: "Even if I should come to you and ask you to see me, I beg you not to do it.'

"My people thought he had got entangled with some other girl, and were furious with him for jilting me, but I believe there is something more in it than that. I wrote to him, but could get no answer, and I had come to the conclusion that I must try and put the whole thing out of my life, when he suddenly turned up again. Now, this is where the queer part comes in.

"We heard the fowls shrieking one night, and thought a fox was after them. My brothers turned out armed with golf clubs, and I went too. When we got to the hen-house we found several fowl with their throats torn as if a rat had been at them; but the boys discovered that the hen-house door had been forced open, a thing no rat could do. They said a gipsy must have been trying to steal the birds, and told me to go back to the house. I was returning by way of the shrubberies when someone suddenly stepped out in front of me. It was quite light, for the moon was nearly full, and I recognized Donald. He held out his arms and I went to him, but, instead of kissing me, he suddenly bent his head and—look!"

She drew her scarf from her neck and showed us a semicircle of little blue marks on the skin just under the ear, the unmistakable print of human teeth.

"He was after the jugular," said Taverner; "lucky for you he did not break the skin."

"I said to him: 'Donald, what are you doing?' My voice seemed to bring him to himself, and he let me go and tore off through the bushes. The boys chased him but did not catch him, and we have never seen him since."

"You have informed the police, I suppose?" said Taverner.

7

"Father told them someone had tried to rob the hen-roost, but they do not know who it was. You see, I did not tell them I had seen Donald."

"And you walk about the moors by yourself, knowing that he may be lurking in the neighborhood?"

She nodded.

"I should advise you not to, Miss Wynter; the man is probably exceedingly dangerous, especially to you. We will send you back in the car."

"You think he has gone mad? That is exactly what I think. I believe he knew he was going mad, and that was why he broke off our engagement. Dr. Taverner, is there nothing that can be done for him? It seems to me that Donald is not mad in the ordinary way. We had a house-maid once who went off her head, and the whole of her seemed to be insane, if you can understand; but with Donald it seems as if only a little bit of him were crazy, as if his insanity were outside himself. Can you grasp what I mean?"

"It seems to me you have given a very clear description of a case of psychic interference—what was known in scriptural days as 'being possessed by a devil,'" said Taverner.

"Can you do anything for him?" the girl inquired eagerly.

"I may be able to do a good deal if you can get him to come to me."

On our next day at the Harley Street consulting-room we found that the butler had booked an appointment for a Captain Donald Craigie. We discovered him to be a personality of singular charm—one of those highly-strung, imaginative men who have the makings of an artist in them. In his normal state he must have been a delightful companion, but as he faced us across the consulting-room desk he was a man under a cloud.

"I may as well make a clean breast of this matter," he said. "I suppose Beryl told you about their chickens?"

8

"She told us that you tried to bite her."

"Did she tell you I bit the chickens?"

"No."

"Well, I did."

Silence fell for a moment. Then Taverner broke it.

"When did this trouble first start?"

"After I got shell shock. I was blown right out of a trench, and it shook me up pretty badly. I thought I had got off lightly, for I was only in hospital about ten days, but I suppose this is the aftermath."

"Are you one of those people who have a horror of blood?"

"Not especially so. I didn't like it, but I could put up with it. We had to get used to it in the trenches; someone was always getting wounded, even in the quietest times."

"And killed," put in Taverner.

"Yes, and killed," said our patient.

"So you developed a blood hunger?"

"That's about it."

"Underdone meat and all the rest of it, I suppose?"

"No, that is no use to me. It seems a horrible thing to say, but it is fresh blood that attracts me, blood as it comes from the veins of my victim."

"Ah!" said Taverner. "That puts a different complexion on the case."

"I shouldn't have thought it could have been much blacker."

"On the contrary, what you have just told me renders the outlook much more hopeful. You have not so much a blood lust, which might well be an effect of the subconscious mind, as a vitality hunger which is quite a different matter."

Craigie looked up quickly. "That's exactly it. I have never been able to put it into words before, but you have hit the nail on the head."

I saw that my colleague's perspicuity had given him great confidence.

9

"I should like you to come down to my nursing home for a time and be under my personal observation," said Taverner.

"I should like to very much, but I think there is something further you ought to know before I do so. This thing has begun to affect my character. At first it seemed something outside myself, but now I am responding to it, almost helping, and trying to find out ways of gratifying it without getting myself into trouble. That is why I went for the hens when I came down to the Wynters' house. I was afraid I should lose my self-control and go for Beryl. I did in the end, as it happened, so it was not much use. In fact I think it did more harm than good, for I seemed to get into much closer touch with 'It' after I had yielded to the impulse. I know that the best thing I could do would be to do away with myself, but I daren't. I feel that after I am dead I should have to meet—whatever it is—face to face."

"You need not be afraid to come down to the nursing home," said Taverner. "We will look after you."

After he had gone Taverner said to me: "Have you ever heard of vampires, Rhodes?"

"Yes, rather," I said. "I used to read myself to sleep with *Dracula* once when I had a spell of insomnia."

"That," nodding his head in the direction of the departing man, "is a singularly good specimen."

"Do you mean to say you are going to take a revolting case like that down to Hindhead?"

"Not revolting, Rhodes, a soul in a dungeon. The soul may not be very savoury, but it is a fellow creature. Let it out and it will soon clean itself."

I often used to marvel at the wonderful tolerance and compassion Taverner had for erring humanity.

"The more you see of human nature," he said to me once, "the less you feel inclined to condemn it, for you realize how hard it has struggled. No one does wrong because he likes it, but because it is the lesser of the two evils."

10

III

A couple of days later I was called out of the nursing home office to receive a new patient. It was Craigie. He had got as far as the door-mat, and there he had stuck. He seemed so thoroughly ashamed of himself that I had not the heart to administer the judicious bullying which is usual under such circumstances.

"I feel as if I were driving a baulking horse," he said. "I want to come in, but I can't."

I called Taverner and the sight of him seemed to relieve our patient.

"Ah," he said, "you give me confidence. I feel that I can defy 'It,' " and he squared his shoulders and crossed the threshold. Once inside, a weight seemed lifted from his mind, and he settled down quite happily to the routine of the place. Beryl Wynter used to walk over almost every afternoon, unknown to her family, and cheer him up; in fact he seemed on the high road to recovery.

One morning I was strolling round the grounds with the head gardener, planning certain small improvements, when he made a remark to me which I had reason to remember later.

"You would think all the German prisoners should have been returned by now, wouldn't you, sir? But they haven't. I passed one the other night in the lane outside the back door. I never thought that I should see their filthy field-grey again."

I sympathized with his antipathy; he had been a prisoner in their hands, and the memory was not one to fade.

I thought no more of his remark, but a few days later I was reminded of it when one of our patients came to me and said:

"Dr. Rhodes, I think you are exceedingly unpatriotic to employ German prisoners in the garden when so many discharged soldiers cannot get work."

I assured her that we did not do so, no German being

11

likely to survive a day's work under the superintendence of our ex-prisoner head gardener.

"But I distinctly saw the man going round the greenhouses at shutting-up time last night," she declared. "I recognized him by his flat cap and grey uniform."

I mentioned this to Taverner.

"Tell Craigie he is on no account to go out after sundown," he said, "and tell Miss Wynter she had better keep away for the present."

A night or two later, as I was strolling round the grounds smoking an after-dinner cigarette, I met Craigie hurrying through the shrubbery.

"You will have Dr. Taverner on your trail," I called after him.

"I missed the post-bag," he replied, "and I am going down to the pillar-box."

Next evening I again found Craigie in the grounds after dark. I bore down on him.

"Look here, Craigie," I said, "if you come to this place you must keep the rules, and Dr. Taverner wants you to stay indoors after sundown."

Craigie bared his teeth and snarled at me like a dog. I took him by the arm and marched him into the house and reported the incident to Taverner.

"The creature has re-established its influence over him," he said. "We cannot evidently starve it out of existence by keeping it away from him; we shall have to use other methods. Where is Craigie at the present moment?"

"Playing the piano in the drawing-room," I replied.

"Then we will go up to his room and unseal it."

As I followed Taverner upstairs he said to me: "Did it ever occur to you to wonder why Craigie jibbed on the doorstep?"

"I paid no attention," I said. "Such a thing is common enough with mental cases."

"There is a sphere of influence, a kind of psychic belljar, over this house to keep out evil entities, what might in

12

popular language be called a 'spell.' Craigie's familiar could not come inside, and did not like being left behind. I thought we might be able to tire it out by keeping Craigie away from its influences, but it has got too strong a hold over him, and he deliberately co-operates with it. Evil communications corrupt good manners, and you can't keep company with a thing like that and not be tainted, especially if you are a sensitive Celt like Craigie."

When we reached the room Taverner went over to the window and passed his hand across the sill, as if sweeping something aside.

"There," he said. "It can come in now and fetch him out, and we will see what it does."

At the doorway he paused again and made a sign on the lintel.

"I don't think it will pass that," he said.

When I returned to the office I found the village policeman waiting to see me.

"I should be glad if you would keep an eye on your dog, sir," he said. "We have been having complaints of sheep-killing lately, and whatever animal is doing it is working in a three-mile radius with this as the centre."

"Our dog is an Airedale," I said. "I should not think he is likely to be guilty. It is usually collies that take to sheep-killing."

At eleven o'clock we turned out the lights and herded our patients off to bed. At Taverner's request I changed into an old suit and rubber-soled tennis shoes and joined him in the smoking-room, which was under Craigie's bedroom. We sat in the darkness awaiting events.

"I don't want you to do anything," said Taverner, "but just to follow and see what happens."

We had not long to wait.

In about a quarter-of-an-hour we heard a rustling in the creepers, and down came Craigie hand over fist, swinging himself along by the great ropes of wisteria that clothed the wall. As he disappeared into the shrubbery I slipped

13

after him, keeping in the shadow of the house.

He moved at a stealthy dog-trot over the heather paths towards Frensham.

At first I ran and ducked, taking advantage of every patch of shadow, but presently I saw that this caution was unnecessary. Craigie was absorbed in his own affairs, and thereupon I drew closer to him, following at a distance of some sixty yards.

He moved at a swinging pace, a kind of loping trot that put me in mind of a blood-hound. The wide, empty levels of that forsaken country stretched out on either side of us, belts of mist filled the hollows, and the heights of Hindhead stood out against the stars. I felt no nervousness; man for man, I reckoned I was a match for Craigie, and, in addition, I was armed with what is technically known as a "soother"—two feet of lead gas-piping inserted in a length of rubber hose-pipe. It is not included in the official equipment of the best asylums, but can frequently be found in a keeper's trouser-leg.

If I had known what I had to deal with I should not have put so much reliance on my "soother." Ignorance is sometimes an excellent substitute for courage.

Suddenly out of the heather ahead of us a sheep got up, and then the chase began. Away went Craigie in pursuit, and away went the terrified wether. A sheep can move remarkably fast for a short distance, but the poor wool-encumbered beast could not keep pace, and Craigie ran it down, working in gradually lessening circles. It stumbled, went to its knees, and he was on it. He pulled its head back, and whether he used a knife or not I could not see, for a cloud passed over the moon, but dimly luminous in the shadow, I saw something that was semi-transparent pass between me and the dark, struggling mass among the heather. As the moon cleared the clouds I made out the flat-topped cap and field-grey uniform of the German Army.

I cannot possibly convey the sickening horror of that

14

sight—the creature that was not a man assisting the man who, for the moment, was not human.

Gradually the sheep's struggles weakened and ceased. Craigie straightened his back and stood up; then he set off at his steady lope towards the east, his grey familiar at his heels.

How I made the homeward journey I do not know. I dared not look behind lest I should find a Presence at my elbow; every breath of wind that blew across the heather seemed to be cold fingers on my throat; fir trees reached out long arms to clutch me as I passed under them, and heather bushes rose up and assumed human shapes. I moved like a runner in a nightmare, making prodigious efforts after a receding goal.

At last I tore across the moonlit lawns of the house, regardless who might be looking from the windows, burst into the smoking-room and flung myself face downwards on the sofa.

IV

"Tut, tut!" said Taverner. "Has it been as bad as all that?"

I could not tell him what I had seen, but he seemed to know.

"Which way did Craigie go after he left you?" he asked.

"Towards the moonrise," I told him.

"And you were on the way to Frensham? He is heading for the Wynters' house. This is very serious, Rhodes. We must go after him; it may be too late as it is. Do you feel equal to coming with me?"

He gave me a stiff glass of brandy, and we went to get the car out of the garage. In Taverner's company I felt secure. I could understand the confidence he inspired in his patients. Whatever that grey shadow might be, I felt he could deal with it and that I would be safe in his hands.

We were not long in approaching our destination.

"I think we will leave the car here," said Taverner, turning into a grass-grown lane. "We do not want to rouse them if we can help it."

We moved cautiously over the dew-soaked grass into the paddock that bounded one side of the Wynters' garden. It was separated from the lawn by a sunk fence, and we could command the whole front of the house and easily gain the terrace if we so desired. In the shadow of a rose pergola we paused. The great trusses of bloom, colourless in the moonlight, seemed a ghastly mockery of our business.

For some time we waited, and then a movement caught my eye.

Out in the meadow behind us something was moving at a slow lope; it followed a wide arc, of which the house formed the focus, and disappeared into a little coppice on the left. It might have been imagination, but I thought I saw a wisp of mist at its heels.

We remained where we were, and presently he came round once more, this time moving in a smaller circle—evidently closing in upon the house. The third time he reappeared more quickly, and this time he was between us and the terrace.

"Quick! Head him off," whispered Taverner. "He will be up the creepers next round."

We scrambled up the sunk fence and dashed across the lawn. As we did so a girl's figure appeared at one of the windows; it was Beryl Wynter. Taverner, plainly visible in the moonlight, laid his finger on his lips and beckoned her to come down.

"I am going to do a very risky thing," he whispered, "but she is a girl of courage, and if her nerve does not fail we shall be able to pull it off."

In a few seconds she slipped out of a side door and joined us, a cloak over her nightdress.

"Are you prepared to undertake an exceedingly unpleasant task?" Taverner asked her. "I can guarantee you will be perfectly safe so long as you keep your head, but if you lose your nerve you will be in grave danger."

"Is it to do with Donald?" she inquired.

"It is," said Taverner. "I hope to be able to rid him of the thing that is overshadowing him and trying to obsess him."

"I have seen it," she said; "it is like a wisp of grey vapour that floats just behind him. It has the most awful face you ever saw. It came up to the window last night, just the face only, while Donald was going round and round the house."

"What did you do?" asked Taverner.

"I didn't do anything. I was afraid that if someone found him he might be put in an asylum, and then we should have no chance of getting him well."

Taverner nodded.

" 'Perfect love casteth out fear,' " he said. "You can do the thing that is required of you."

He placed Miss Wynter on the terrace in full moonlight.

"As soon as Craigie sees you," he said, "retreat round the corner of the house into the yard. Rhodes and I will wait for you there."

A narrow doorway led from the terrace to the back premises, and just inside its arch Taverner bade me take my stand.

"Pinion him as he comes past you and hang on for your life," he said. "Only mind he doesn't get his teeth into you; these things are infectious."

We had hardly taken up our positions when we heard the loping trot come round once more, this time on the terrace itself. Evidently he caught sight of Miss Wynter, for the stealthy padding changed to a wild scurry over the gravel, and the girl slipped quickly through the archway and sought refuge behind Taverner. Right on her heels came Craigie. Another yard and he would have had her, but I caught him by the elbows and pinioned him securely. For a moment we swayed and struggled across the dew-

17

drenched flagstones, but I locked him in an old wrestling grip and held him.

"Now," said Taverner, "if you will keep hold of Craigie I will deal with the other. But first of all we must get it away from him, otherwise it will retreat on to him, and he may die of shock. Now, Miss Wynter, are you prepared to play your part?"

"I am prepared to do whatever is necessary," she replied.

Taverner took a scalpel out of a pocket case and made a small incision in the skin of her neck, just under the ear. A drop of blood slowly gathered, showing black in the moonlight.

"That is the bait," he said. "Now go close up to Craigie and entice the creature away; get it to follow you and draw it out into the open."

As she approached us Craigie plunged and struggled in my arms like a wild beast, and then something grey and shadowy drew out of the gloom of the wall and hovered for a moment at my elbow. Miss Wynter came nearer, walking almost into it.

"Don't go too close," cried Taverner, and she paused.

Then the grey shape seemed to make up its mind; it drew clear of Craigie and advanced towards her. She retreated towards Taverner, and the Thing came out into the moonlight. We could see it quite clearly from its flat-topped cap to its knee-boots; its high cheek-bones and slit eyes pointed its origin to the south-eastern corner of Europe where strange tribes still defy civilization and keep up their still stranger beliefs.

The shadowy form drifted onwards, following the girl across the yard, and when it was some twenty feet from Craigie, Taverner stepped out quickly behind it, cutting off its retreat. Round it came in a moment, instantly conscious of his presence, and then began a game of "puss-in-the-corner." Taverner was trying to drive it into a kind of psychic killing-pen he had made for its reception. Invisible to me, the lines of psychic force which bounded it were evidently plainly perceptible to the creature we were hunting. This way and that way it slid in its efforts to escape, but Taverner all the time herded it towards the apex of the invisible triangle, where he could give it its *coup de grace*.

Then the end came. Taverner leapt forward. There was a Sign then a Sound. The grey form commenced to spin like a top. Faster and faster it went, its outlines merging into a whirling spiral of mist; then it broke. Out into space went the particles that had composed its form, and with the almost soundless shriek of supreme speed the soul went to its appointed place.

Then something seemed to lift. From a cold hell of limitless horror the flagged space became a normal back yard, the trees ceased to be tentacled menaces, the gloom of the wall was no longer an ambuscade, and I knew that never again would a grey shadow drift out of the darkness upon its horrible hunting.

I released Craigie, who collapsed in a heap at my feet: Miss Wynter went to rouse her father, while Taverner and I got the insensible man into the house.

What masterly lies Taverner told to the family I have never known, but a couple of months later we received, instead of the conventional fragment of wedding cake, a really substantial chunk, with a note from the bride to say it was to go in the office cupboard, where she knew we kept provisions for those nocturnal meals that Taverner's peculiar habits imposed upon us.

It was during one of these midnight repasts that I questioned Taverner about the strange matter of Craigie and his familiar. For a long time I had not been able to refer to it; the memory of that horrible sheep-killing was a thing that would not bear recalling.

"You have heard of vampires," said Taverner. "That was a typical case. For close on a hundred years they have been practically unknown in Europe—Western Europe

19

that is—but the War has caused a renewed outbreak, and quite a number of cases have been reported.

"When they were first observed—that is to say, when some wretched lad was caught attacking the wounded, they took him behind the lines and shot him, which is not a satisfactory way of dealing with a vampire, unless you also go to the trouble of burning his body, according to the good old-fashioned way of dealing with practitioners of black magic. Then our enlightened generation came to the conclusion that they were not dealing with a crime, but with a disease, and put the unfortunate individual afflicted with this horrible obsession into an asylum, where he did not usually live very long, the supply of his peculiar nourishment being cut off. But it never struck anybody that they might be dealing with more than one factor— that what they were really contending with was a gruesome partnership between the dead and the living."

"What in the world do you mean?" I asked.

"We have two physical bodies, you know," said Taverner, "the dense material one, with which we are all familiar, and the subtle etheric one, which inhabits it, and acts as the medium of the life forces, whose functioning would explain a very great deal if science would only condescend to investigate it. When a man dies, the etheric body, with his soul in it, draws out of the physical form and drifts about in its neighborhood for about three days, or until decomposition sets in, and then the soul draws out of the etheric body also, which in turn dies, and the man enters upon the first phase of his post mortem existence, the purgatorial one.

"Now, it is possible to keep the etheric body together almost indefinitely if a supply of vitality is available, but, having no stomach which can digest food and turn it into energy, the thing has to batten on someone who has, and develops into a spirit parasite which we call a vampire.

"There is a pretty good working knowledge of black magic in Eastern Europe. Now, supposing some man who

20

has this knowledge gets shot, he knows that in three days time, at the death of the etheric body, he will have to face his reckoning, and with his record he naturally does not want to do it, so he establishes a connection with the subconscious mind of some other soul that still has a body, provided he can find one suitable for his purposes. A very positive type of character is useless; he has to find one of a negative type, such as the lower class of medium affords. Hence one of the many dangers of mediumship to the untrained. Such a negative condition may be temporarily induced by, say, shell-shock, and it is possible then for such a soul as we are considering to obtain an influence over a being of much higher type—Craigie, for instance—and use him as a means of obtaining its gratification."

"But why did not the creature confine its attentions to Craigie, instead of causing him to attack others?"

"Because Craigie would have been dead in a week if it had done so, and then it would have found itself minus its human feeding bottle. Instead of that it worked *through* Craigie, getting him to draw extra vitality from others and pass it on to itself; hence it was that Craigie had a vitality hunger rather than a blood hunger, though the fresh blood of a victim was the means of absorbing the vitality."

"Then that German we all saw—?"

"Was merely a corpse who was insufficiently dead."

The Return of the Ritual

It was Taverner's custom, at certain times and seasons, to do what I should call hypnotize himself; he, however, called it "going subconscious," and declared that, by means of concentration, he shifted the focus of his attention from the external world to the world of thought. Of the different states of consciousness to which he thus obtained access, and of the work that could be performed in each one, he would talk by the hour, and I soon learnt to recognize the phases he passed through during this extraordinary process.

Night after night I have watched beside the unconscious body of my colleague as it lay twitching on the sofa while thoughts that were not derived from his mind influenced the passive nerves. Many people can communicate with each other by means of thought, but I had never realized the extent to which this power was employed until I heard Taverner use his body as the receiving instrument of such messages.

One night while he was drinking some hot coffee I had given him (for he was always chilled to the bone after these performances) he said to me: "Rhodes, there is a very curious affair afoot."

I inquired what he meant.

"I am not quite sure," he replied. "There is something going on which I do not understand, and I want you to help me to investigate it."

I promised my assistance, and asked the nature of the problem.

"I told you when you joined me," he said, "that I was a member of an occult brotherhood, but I did not tell you anything about it, because I am pledged not to do so, but for the purpose of our work together I am going to use my discretion and explain certain things to you.

"You know, I daresay, that we make use of ritual in our work. This is not the nonsense you may think it to be, for ritual has a profound effect on the mind. Anyone who is sufficiently sensitive can feel vibrations radiating whenever an occult ceremonial is being performed. For instance, I have only got to listen mentally for a moment to tell whether one of the Lhassa Lodges is working its terrific ritual.

"When I was subconscious just now I heard one of the rituals of my own Order being worked, but worked as no Lodge I have ever sat in would perform it. It was like a rendering of Tschaikowsky picked out on the piano with one finger by a child, and unless I am very much mistaken, some unauthorized person has got hold of that ritual and is experimenting with it."

"Someone has broken his oath and given away your secrets," I said.

"Evidently," said Taverner. "It has not often been done, but instances have occurred, and if any of the Black Lodges, who would know how to make use of it, should get hold of the ritual the results might be serious, for there is great power in these old ceremonies, and while that power is safe in the hands of the carefully picked students whom we initiate, it would be a very different matter in those of unscrupulous men."

"Shall you try to trace it?" I inquired.

"Yes," said Taverner, "but it is easier said than done. I have absolutely nothing to guide me. All I can do is to send round word among the Lodges to see whether a copy is missing from their archives; that will narrow our zone of search somewhat."

Whether Taverner made use of the post or of his own peculiar methods of communication I do not know, but in a few days's time he had the information he required. None of the carefully guarded rituals was missing from any of

23

the Lodges, but when search was made among the records at headquarters it was discovered that a ritual had been stolen from the Florentine Lodge during the middle ages by the custodian of the archives and sold (it was believed) to the Medici; at any rate, it was known to have been worked in Florence during the latter half of the fifteenth century. What became of it after the Medician manuscripts were dispersed at the plundering of Florence by the French was never known; it was lost sight of and was believed to have been destroyed. Now, however, after the lapse of so many centuries someone was waking its amazing power.

As we were passing down Harley Street a few days later, Taverner asked me if I would mind turning aside with him into the Marylebone Lane, where he wished to call at a secondhand bookshop. I was surprised that a man of the type of my colleague should patronize such a place, for it appeared to be stocked chiefly with tattered papercovered Ouidas and out-of-date piousness, and the alacrity with which the shopboy went to fetch the owner showed that my companion was a regular and esteemed customer.

The owner when he appeared was an even greater surprise than his shop; unbelievably dusty, his frock-coat, beard and face all appeared to be of a uniform grey-green, yet when he spoke his voice was that of a cultured man, and, though my companion addressed him as an equal, he answered as to a superior.

"Have you received any reply to the advertisement I asked you to insert for me?" asked Taverner of the snuff-coloured individual who confronted us.

"I have not; but I have got some information for you— you are not the only purchaser in the market for the manuscript."

"My competitor being?"

"A man named Williams."

"That does not tell us very much."

"The postmark was Chelsea," said the old bookseller with a significant look.

"Ah!" said my employer. "If that manuscript should come into the market I will not limit you as to price."

"I think we are likely to have a little excitement" observed Taverner as we left the shop, its dust-covered occupant bowing behind us. "The Chelsea Black Lodges have evidently heard what I heard and are also making a bid for the ritual."

"You do not suppose that it is one of the Chelsea Lodges that has got it at the present moment?" I inquired.

"I do not," said Taverner, "for they would have made a better job of it. Whatever may be said against their morals, they are not fools, and know what they are about. No, some person or group of persons who dabbles in the occult without any real knowledge has got hold of that manuscript. They know enough to recognize a ritual when they see it, and are playing about with it to see what will happen. Probably no one would be more astonished than they if anything *did* happen.

"Were the ritual confined to such hands as those I should not be worried about it; but it may get into the possession of people who will know how to use it and abuse its powers, and then the consequences will be much more serious than you can realize. I will even go so far as to say that the course of civilization would be effected if such a thing occurred."

I saw that Taverner was profoundly moved. Regardless of traffic he plunged into the roadway, making a bee-line for his rooms.

"I would give any price for that manuscript if I could lay my hands on it, and if it were not for sale I would not hesitate to steal it; but how in the name of Heaven am I to trace the thing?"

We had regained the consulting-room, and Taverner was pacing up and down the floor with long strides. Presently he took up the telephone and rang up his Hindhead nursing home and told the matron that we should be spending the night in Town. As there was no sleeping accommodation at the house in Harley Street, where he had his London headquarters, I guessed that a night of vigil was in contemplation.

I was fairly used to these watch-nights now; I knew that my duty would be to guard Taverner's vacated body while his soul ranged through outer darkness on some strange quest of its own and talked to its peers—men who were also able to leave their bodies at will and walk the starry ways with him, or others who had died centuries ago, but were still concerned with the welfare of their fellow men whom they had lived to serve.

We dined at a little restaurant in a back street off Soho, where the head waiter argued metaphysics in Italian with Taverner between courses, and returned to our Harley Street quarters to wait until the great city about us should have gone to sleep and left the night quiet for the work we were about to embark upon. It was not till well after midnight that Taverner judged the time was suitable, and then he settled himself upon the broad consulting-room couch, with myself at his feet.

In a few minutes he was asleep, but as I watched him I saw his breathing alter, and sleep gave way to trance. A few muttered words, stray memories of his previous earthly lives, came from his lips; then a deep and sibilant breath marked a second change of level, and I saw that he was in the state of consciousness that occultists use when they communicate with each other by means of telepathy. It was exactly like "listening in" with a wireless telephone; Lodge called to Lodge across the deeps of the night, and the passive brain picked up the vibrations and passed them on to the voice, and Taverner spoke.

The jangle of messages, however, was cut off in the middle of a sentence. This was not the level on which Taverner meant to work to-night. Another sibilant hiss announced that he had gone yet deeper into the hypnotic condition. There was a dead stillness in the room, and then a voice that was not Taverner's broke the silence.

26

"The level of the Records," it said, and I guessed what Taverner meant to do; no brain but his could have hit upon the extraordinary scheme of tracing the manuscript by examining the subconscious mind of the human race. Taverner, in common with his fellow psychologists, held that every thought and every act have their images stored in the person's subconscious mind, but he also held that records of them are stored in the mind of Nature; and it was these records that he was seeking to read.

Broken fragments of sentences, figures, and names, fell from the lips of the unconscious man, and then he got his focus and steadied to his work.

*"Il cinquecento, Firenze, Italia, Pierro della Costa."** came a deep level voice; then followed a long-drawn out vibrating sound half-way between a telephone bell and the note of a 'cello, and the voice changed.

"Two forty-five, November the fourteenth, 1898, London, England."

For a time there was silence, but almost immediately Taverner's voice cut across it.

"I want Pierro della Costa, who was reborn November the fourteenth, 1898, at two forty-five a.m."

Silence. And then Taverner's voice again calling as if over a telephone: "Hullo! Hullo! Hullo!" Apparently he received an answer, for his tone changed. "Yes; it is the Senior of Seven who is speaking."

Then his voice took on an extraordinary majesty and command.

"Brother, where is the ritual that was entrusted to thy care?"

What answer was given I could not divine; but after a pause Taverner's voice came again. "Brother, redeem thy crime and return the ritual whence it was taken." Then he rolled over on to his side, and the trance condition passed into natural sleep, and so to an awakening.

*"The fifteenth century, Florence, Italy, Peter della Costa."

Dazed and shivering, he recovered consciousness, and I gave him hot coffee from a Thermos flask, such as we always kept handy for these midnight meals. I recounted to him what had passed, and he nodded his satisfaction between sips of the steaming liquid.

"I wonder how Pierro della Costa will effect his task," he said. "The present day personality will probably not have the faintest idea as to what is required of it, and will be blindly urged forward by the subconscious."

"How will it locate the manuscript?" I inquired. "Why should he succeed where you failed?"

"I failed because I could not at any point establish contact with the manuscript. I was not on earth at the time it was stolen, and I could not trace it in the racial memories for the same reason. One must have a jumping-off place, you know. Occult work is not performed by merely waving a wand."

"How will the present day Pierro go to work?" I inquired.

"The present day Pierro won't do anything," said Taverner, "because he does not know how, but his subconscious mind is that of the trained occultist, and under the stimulus I have given it, will perform its work; it will probably go back to the time when the manuscript was handed over to the Medici, and then trace its subsequent history by means of the racial memories—the subconscious memory of Nature."

"And how will he go to work to recover it?"

"As soon as the subconscious has located its quarry, it will send an impulse through into the conscious mind, bidding it take the body upon the quest, and a very puzzled modern young man may find himself in a difficult situation."

"How will he know what to do with the manuscript when he has found it?"

"Once an Initiate, always an Initiate. In all moments of difficulty and danger the Initiate turns to his Master. Something in that boy's soul will reach out to make contact, and he will be brought back to his own Fraternity. Sooner or later he will come across one of the Brethren, who will know what to do with him."

I was thankful enough to lie down on the sofa and get a couple of hours' sleep, until such time as the charwoman should disturb me; but Taverner, upon whom "going subconscious" always seemed to have the effect of a tonic, announced his intention of seeing the sun rise from London Bridge, and left me to my own devices.

He returned in time to take me out to breakfast, and I discovered that he had given instructions for every morning paper and each successive edition of the evening ones to be sent in to us. All day long the stream of printed matter poured in, and had to be gone over, for Taverner was on the lookout for Pierro della Costa's effort to recover the ritual.

"His first attempt upon it is certain to be some blind lunatic outburst," said Taverner, "and it will probably land him in the hands of the police, whence it will be our duty as good Brethren, to rescue him; but it will have served its purpose, for he will, as it were, have 'pointed' the manuscript after the fashion of a sporting dog."

Next morning our vigilance was rewarded. An unusual case of attempted burglary was reported from St. John's Wood. A young bank clerk of hitherto exemplary character, had effected an entry into the house of a Mr. Joseph Coates by the simple expedient of climbing on to the dining-room window-sill from the area steps, and, in full view of the entire street, kicking the glass out of the window. Mr. Coates, aroused by the din, came down armed with a stick, which, however, was not required. The would-be burglar (who could give no explanation of his conduct) was meekly waiting to be taken to the police station by the policeman who had been attracted to the spot by the commotion he had made.

Taverner immediately telephoned to find out what time the case would be coming on at the police court, and we forthwith set out upon our quest. We sat in the enclosure reserved for the general public while various cases of wife-beaters and disorderly drunkards were disposed of, and I watched my neighbors.

Not far from us a girl of a different type from the rest of the sordid audience was seated; her pale oval face seemed to belong to another race from the irregular Cockney features about her. She looked like some mediaeval saint from an Italian fresco, and it only needed the stiff bro-caded robes to complete the resemblance.

" 'Look for the woman,' " said Taverner's voice in my ear. "Now we know why Pierro della Costa fell to a bribe."

The usual riff-raff having been dealt with, a prisoner of a different type was placed in the dock. A young fellow, re-fined, highly strung, looked round him in bewilderment at his unaccustomed surroundings, and then, catching sight of the olive-cheeked madonna in the gallery, took heart of grace.

He answered the magistrate's questions collectedly enough, giving his name as Peter Robson, and his pro-fession as clerk. He listened attentively to the evidence of the policeman who had arrested him, and to Mr. Joseph Coates, and when asked for his explanation, said he had none to give. In answer to questions, he declared that he had never been in that part of London before; he had no motive for going there, and he did not know why he had attempted to enter the window.

The magistrate, who at first had seemed disposed to deal leniently with the case, appeared to think that this persist-ent refusal of all explanation must conceal some motive, and proceeded to press the prisoner somewhat sharply. It looked as if matters were going hard with him, when Taverner, who had been scribbling on the back of a visit-ing card, beckoned an usher and sent the message up to the magistrate. I saw him read it, and turn the card over. Taverner's degrees and the Harley Street address were enough for him.

"I understand," said he to the prisoner, "that you have a friend here who can offer an explanation of the affair, and is prepared to go surety for you."

The prisoner's face was a study; he looked round, seeking some familiar face, and when Taverner, well-dressed and of imposing appearance, entered the witness box, his perplexity was comical; and then, through all his bewilderment, a flash of light suddenly shot into the boy's eyes. Some gleam from the subconscious reached him, and he shut his mouth and awaited events.

My colleague, giving his name as John Richard Taverner, doctor of medicine, philosophy and science, master of arts and bachelor at law, said that he was a distant relation of the prisoner who was subject to that peculiar malady known as double personality. He was satisfied that this condition was quite sufficient to account for the attempt at burglary, some freak of the boy's other self having led to the crime.

Yes, Taverner was quite prepared to go surety for the boy, and the magistrate, evidently relieved at the turn affairs had taken, forthwith bound the prisoner over to come up for judgment if called upon, and within ten minutes of Taverner's entry upon the scene we were standing on the steps of the court, where the Florentine madonna joined us.

"I don't know who you are, sir," the boy was saying, "nor why you should help me, but I am very grateful to you. May I introduce my *fiancee*, Miss Fenner? She would like to thank you, too."

Taverner shook hands with the girl.

"I don't suppose you two have eaten much breakfast with this affair hanging over your heads," he said. They admitted that they had not.

"Then," said he, "you must be my guests for an early lunch."

We all packed into a taxi, and drove to the restaurant where the metaphysical head waiter held sway. Here Peter

31

Robson immediately tackled Taverner.

"Look here, sir," he said, "I am exceedingly grateful to you for what you have done for me, but I should very much like to know why you did it."

"Do you ever weave daydreams?" inquired Taverner irrelevantly. Robson stared at him in perplexity, but the girl at his side suddenly exclaimed:

"I know what you mean. Do you remember, Peter, the stories we used to make up when we were children? How we belonged to a secret society that had it headquarters in the woodshed, and had only to make a certain sign and people would know we were members and be afraid of us? I remember once, when we had been locked in the scullery because we were naughty, you said that if you made this sign, the policeman would come in and tell your father he had got to let us out, because we belonged to a powerful Brotherhood that did not allow its members to be locked in sculleries. That is exactly what has happened; it is your daydream come true. But what is the meaning of it all?"

"Ah, what, indeed?" said Taverner. Then turning to the boy: "Do you dream much?" he asked.

"Not as a rule," he replied, "but I had a most curious dream the night before last, which I can only regard as prophetic in light of subsequent events. I dreamt that someone was accusing me of a crime, and I woke up in a dreadful way about it."

"Dreams are curious things," said Taverner, "both day dreams and night dreams. I don't know which are the stranger. Do you belive in the immortality of the soul, Mr. Robson?'

"Of course I do."

"Then has it ever struck you the eternal life must stretch both ways?"

"You mean," said Robson under his breath, "that it wasn't all imagination. It might be—memory?"

"Other people have had the same dream," said Taverner, "myself among them." Then he leant across the narrow table and stared into the lad's eyes.

"Supposing I told you that just such an organization as you imagined exists; that if, as a boy even, you had gone out into the main street and made that Sign, someone would have been almost certain to answer it?

"Supposing I told you that the impulse which made you break that window was not a blind instinct, but an attempt to carry out an order from your Fraternity, would you believe me?"

"I think I should," said the lad opposite him. "At any rate, if it isn't true, I wish it were, for it appeals to me more than anything I have ever heard."

"If you care to go deeper into the matter," said Taverner, "will you come this evening to my place in Harley Street, and then we can talk the matter over?"

Robson accepted with eagerness. What man would refuse to follow his daydreams when they began to materialize?

After we had parted from our new acquaintance, we took a taxi to St. John's Wood and stopped at a house whose front ground floor window was in process of being reglazed. Taverner sent in his card, and we were ushered into a room decorated with large bronze Buddhas, statuettes from Egyptian tombs, and pictures by Watts. In a few minutes Mr. Coates appeared.

"Ah, Dr. Taverner," he said, "I presume you have come about the extraordinary matter of your young relative who broke into my house last evening?"

"That is so, Mr. Coates," replied my companion. "I have come to offer you my sincere apologies on behalf of the family."

"Don't mention it," said our host, "the poor lad was suffering from mental trouble, I take it?"

"A passing mania," said Taverner, brushing it away with a wave of his hand. He glanced round the room. "I see by your books that you are interested in a hobby of my own, the ancient mystery religions. I think I may claim to be something of an Egyptologist."

Coates rose to the bait at once.

"I came across the most extraordinary document the other day," said our new acquaintance. "I should like to show it to you. I think you would be interested."

He drew from his pocket a bunch of keys, and inserted one in the lock of a drawer in a bureau. To his astonishment the key pushed loosely through the hole, and he pulled the drawer open only to find that the lock had been forced off. He ran his hand to the back of the drawer, and withdrew it empty! Coates looked from Taverner to myself and back again in astonishment.

"That manuscript was there when I went to the police court this morning," he said. "What is the meaning of this extraordinary business? First of all a man breaks into my house and makes no attempt to steal anything, and then someone else breaks in and, neglecting many objects of value, takes a thing that can be of no interest to anyone but myself."

"Then the manuscript which has been stolen is of no particular value?" said Taverner.

"I gave half-a-crown for it," replied Coates.

"Then you should be thankful to have got off so light," said Taverner.

"This is the devil, Rhodes," he went on, as we reentered the waiting taxi. "Someone from a Chelsea Black Lodge, knowing Coates would be at the police court this morning, has taken that manuscript."

"What is to be the next move?" I inquired.

"Get hold of Robson; we can only work through him."

I asked him how he intended to deal with the situation that had arisen.

"Are you going to send Robson after the manuscript again?" I inquired.

"I shall have to," said Taverner.

"I do not think there is the makings of a successful buccaneer in Robson."

"Neither do I," agreed Taverner; "we shall have to fall back on Pierro della Costa."

Robson met us at Harley Street, and Taverner took him out to dinner.

After dinner we returned to the consulting room, where Taverner handed round cigars, and set himself to be an agreeable host, a task in which he succeeded to perfection, for he was one of the most interesting talkers I have ever met.

Presently the talk led round to Italy during the Renaissance, and the great days of Florence and the Medici; and then he began to tell the story of one, Pierro della Costa, who had been a student of the occult arts in those days, and had brewed love philtres for the ladies of the Florentine court. He told the story with considerable vividness, and in great detail, and I was surprised to see that the attention of the lad was wandering, and that he was apparently pursuing a train of thought of his own, oblivious of his surroundings. Then I realized that he was sliding off into that trance condition with which my experience of my colleague had made me familiar.

Still Taverner talked on, telling the history of the old Florentine to the unconscious boy—how he rose to be custodian of the archives, was offered a bribe, and betrayed his trust in order that he might buy the favour of the woman he loved. Then, as he came to the end of the story, his voice changed, and he addressed the unconscious lad by name.

"Pierro della Costa," he said, "why did you do it?"

"Because I was tempted," came the answer, but not in the voice in which the boy had talked to us; it was a man's voice, calm, deep, and dignified, vibrating with emotion.

"Do you regret it?" asked Taverner.

"I do," returned the voice that was not the boy's voice. "I have asked of the Great Ones that I may be permitted to restore that which I stole."

"Thy request is granted," said Taverner. "Do that which

thou hast to do, and the blessing of the Great Ones be upon thee."

Slowly the boy rolled over and sat up, but I saw at a glance that it was not the same individual who confronted us: a man, mature, of strong character and determined purpose, looked out of the boy's blue eyes.

"I go," he said, "to restore that which I took. Give me the means."

We went round, he and Taverner and I, to the garage, and got out the car. "Which way do you want to go?" asked my colleague. The lad pointed to the south-west, and Taverner turned the car in the direction of the Marble Arch. Piloted by the man who was not Robson, we went south down Park Lane, and finally came out in the tangle of mean streets behind Victoria Station; thence we turned east. We pulled up behind the Tate Gallery, and the boy got out.

"From here," he said, "I go on alone," and he disappeared down a side street.

Although we waited for a matter of half-an-hour, Taverner did not stop the engine. "We may want to get out of here quick," he said. Then, just as I was beginning to wonder if we were going to spend the night in the open, we heard running footsteps coming down the street, and Robson leapt into the car. That Taverner's precaution in not stopping the engine was justified was proved by the fact that close upon Robson's heels other footsteps sounded.

"Quick, Rhodes," cried Taverner. "Hang the rug over the back." I did as I was bid, and succeeded in obscuring the number plate, and as the first of our pursuers rounded the corner, the big car leapt into its stride, and we drew clear.

No one spoke on the journey to Hindhead.

We entered the sleeping house as quietly as might be, and as Taverner turned on the office lights, I saw that Robson carried a curious looking volume bound in vellum.

We did not tarry in the office, however, for Taverner led us through the sleeping house to a door which I knew led down to the cellar stairs.

"Come too, Rhodes," said Taverner. "You have seen the beginning of this matter, and you shall see the end, for you have shared in the risk, and although you are not one of Us, I know that I can rely on your discretion."

We passed down the spiral stone stairs and along a flagged passage. Taverner unlocked a door, and admitted us to a wine cellar. He crossed this, and unlocked a further door. A dim point of flame illumined the darkness ahead of us, swaying uneasily in the draught. Taverner turned on a light, and to my intense surprise I found myself in a chapel. High carved stalls were built into the walls on three sides, and on the fourth was an altar. The flickering light I had seen in the darkness came from the floating wick of a lamp hung above our heads as the centre point of a great Symbol.

Taverner lit the incense in a bronze thurible, and set it swinging. He handed Robson the black robe of an Inquisitor, and he himself assumed another one; then these two cowled figures faced one another across the floor of the empty chapel. Taverner began what was evidently a prayer. I could not gather its substance, for I am unable to follow spoken Latin. Then came a Litany of question and response, Robson, the London clerk, answering in the deep resonant voice of a man accustomed to intone across great buildings. Then he rose to his feet, and with the stately steps of a processional advanced to the altar, and laid thereon the ragged and mildewed manuscript he held in his hands. He knelt, and what absolution the sombre figure that stood over him pronounced, I cannot tell, but he rose to his feet like a man from whose shoulders a great burden has been rolled.

Then for the first time, Taverner spoke in his native tongue. "In all moments of difficulty and danger"—the booming of his deep voice filled the room with echoes—

37

"make this Sign." And I knew that the man who had betrayed his trust had made good and been received back into his old Fraternity.

We returned to the upper world, and the man who was not Robson bade us farewell. "It is necessary that I should go," he said.

"It is indeed," said Taverner. "You had better be out of England till this matter has blown over. Rhodes, will you undertake to drive him down to Southampton? I have other work to do."

As we dropped down the long slope that leads to Liphook, I studied the man at my side. By some strange alchemy Taverner had woken the long dead soul of Pierro della Costa and imposed it upon the present day personality of Peter Robson. Power radiated from him as light from a lamp; even the features seemed changed. Deep lines about the corners of the mouth lent a firmness to the hitherto indefinite chin, and the light blue eyes, now sunken in the head, had taken on the glitter of steel and were as steady as those of a swordsman.

It was just after six in the morning when we crossed the floating bridge into Southampton. The place was already astir, for a dock town never sleeps, and we inquired our way to the little-known inn where Taverner had directed us to go for breakfast. We discovered it to be an unpretentious public house near the dock gates, and the potman was just drawing the bright curtains of turkey twill as we entered.

It was evident that strangers were not very welcome in the little tavern, and no one offered to take our order. As we stood there irresolute, heavy footsteps thundered down creaking wooden stairs, and a strongly built man wearing the four lines of gold braid denoting the rank of Captain entered the bar parlour. He glanced at us as he came in, and indeed we were sufficiently incongruous to be notable in such a place.

His eyes attracted my attention; he had the keen, out-looking gaze so characteristic of a seaman, but in addition to this he had a curious trick of looking at one without appearing to see one; the focus of the eyes met about a yard behind one's back. It was a thing I had often seen Taverner do when he wished to see the colours of an aura, that curious emanation which, for those who can see it, radiates from every living thing and is so clear an indication of the condition within.

Grey eyes looked into blue as the newcomer took in my companion, and then an almost imperceptible sign passed between them, and the sailor joined us.

"I believe you know my mother," he remarked by way of introduction. Robson admitted the acquaintanceship, though I am prepared to swear he had never seen the man before, and we all three adjourned to an inner room for breakfast, which appeared in response to the bellowed orders of our new acquaintance.

Without any preamble he inquired our business, and Robson was equally ready to communicate it.

"I want to get out of the country as quietly as possible," he said. Our new friend seemed to think that it was quite in the ordinary course of events that a man without luggage should be departing in this manner.

"I am sailing at nine this morning, going down the Gold Coast as far as Loango. We aren't exactly the Cunard, but if you care to come you will be welcome. You can't wear that rig, however; you would only draw a crowd, which I take is what you don't want to do."

He put his head through a half-door which separated the parlour from the back premises, and in response to his vociferations a little fat man with white chin whiskers appeared. A consultation took place between the two, the newcomer being equally ready to lend his assistance. Very shortly a suit of cheap serge reach-me-downs and a peaked cap were forthcoming, these being, the sailor assured us, the correct costume for a steward, in which capacity it was designed that Peter Robson should go to sea.

Leaving the inn that the mysterious Fellowship had made so hospitable to us, we took our way to the docks, and passing through the wilderness of railway lines, cranes, and yawning gulfs that constitute their scenery, we arrived at our companion's ship, a rusty-side tramp, her upper works painted a dirty white.

We accompanied her captain to his cabin, a striking contrast to the raffle outside: a solid desk bearing a student's shaded lamp, a copy of Albrercht Durer's study of the *Praying Hands*, a considerable shelf of books, and, perceptible beneath the all-pervading odour of strong tobacco, the faint spicy smell that clings to a place where incense is regularly burnt. I studied the titles of the books, for they tell one more of a man than anything else; *Isis Unveiled* stood cheek by jowl with *Creative Evolution* and two fat tomes of Eliphas Levi's *History of Magic*.

On the drive back to Hindhead I thought much of the strange side of life with which I had come in contact.

Yet another example was afforded me of the widespread ramifications of the Society. At Taverner's request I looked up the sea captain on his return from the voyage and asked him for news of Robson. This he was unable to give me, however; he had put the lad ashore at some mudhole on the West Coast. Standing on the quay stewing in the sunshine he had made the Sign. A half-caste Portuguese had touched him on the shoulder, and the two had vanished in the crowd. I expressed some anxiety as to the fate of an inexperienced lad in a strange land.

"You needn't worry," said the sailor. "That Sign would take him right across Africa and back again."

When I was talking the matter over with Taverner, I said to him: "What made you and the captain claim relationship with Robson? It seemed to me a perfectly gratuitous lie."

"It was no lie, but the truth," said Taverner. "Who is my Mother, and who are my Brethren but the Lodge and the initiates thereof?"

The Man Who Sought

One of Taverner's cases will always stand out in my mind—the case of Black, the airman. The ordinary doctor would have bromided Black into an asylum, but Taverner staked the sanity of two people upon a theory, and saved them both.

Early in May I was sitting with him in his Harley Street consulting-room, taking down case notes while he examined his patients. We had dispatched various hysterics and neurotics to other specialists for treatment, when a man of an entirely different type was ushered in by the butler. He looked absolutely healthy, his face was tanned with the open air and had no sign of nervous tension; but when I met his eyes I noticed something unusual about them. The expression was peculiar. They did not hold the haunting fear one so often sees in the eyes of the mentally sick; he reminded me of nothing in the world but a running hound that has sighted its prey.

"I think I am going off my head," announced our visitor.

"What form does your trouble take?" inquired Taverner.

"Can't do my work. Can't sit still. Can't do a thing except tear all over the country in my car as hard as ever I can lick. Look at my endorsements." He held out a driving license filled with writing. "Next time they'll quod me, and that will finish me off altogether. If they shut me up inside four walls I'll buzz around like a cockchafer in a bottle till I knock myself to pieces. I'd go clean mad if I couldn't move about. The only relief I get is speed, to feel that I am going somewhere. I drive and drive and drive till I'm clean tuckered out, and then I roll into the nearest wayside pub and sleep; but it doesn't do me any good, because I only dream, and that seems to make things more real, and I wake up madder than ever and go on driving again."

"What is your work?" said Taverner.

"Motor-racing and flying."

"Are you Arnold Black, by any chance?" asked Taverner.

"That's me," said our patient. "Praise the Lord I haven't lost my nerve yet."

"You had a crash a little while ago, did you not?" inquired my colleague.

"That was what started the trouble," said Black. "I was all right till then. Banged my head, I suppose. I was unconscious three days, and when I came round I was seedy, and have been so ever since."

I thought Taverner would refuse the case, for an ordinary head injury could have little interest for him, but instead he asked: "What made you come to me?"

"I was on my beam ends," said Black. "I'd been to two or three old ducks, but could get no sense out of them; in fact I've just come on from the blankest geyser of the lot." He named a name of eminence. "Told me to stop in bed a month and feed up. I wandered down the road and liked the look of your brass plate, so I came in. Why? Aren't I in your line? What do you go in for? Babies or senile decay?"

"If a chance like that brought you to me, you probably are in my line," said Taverner. "Now tell me the physical side of your case. What do you feel like in yourself?"

Our patient wriggled uneasily in his chair.

"I dunno," he said. "I feel more of a fool than anything else."

"That," said Taverner, "is often the beginning of wisdom."

Black half turned away from us. His painfully assumed jauntiness fell from him. There was a long pause, and then he blurted out:

"I feel as if I were in love."

"And you've been hard hit?" suggested Taverner.

"No, I've not," said the patient. "I'm not in love, I only feel as if I were. There isn't a girl in the case—not that I know of, anyway—and yet I'm in love—horribly in love— with a woman who doesn't exist. And it's not the tomcat side of me, but the biggest and best that there is in me. If I can't get someone to love me back in the same way that I am loving, then I'll go off my head. All the time I feel that there must be someone somewhere, and that she'll sud- denly turn up. She *must* turn up." His jaw set in a savage line. "That's why I drive so much, because I feel that round the next bend I'll find her."

The man's face was quivering, and I saw that his hands were wet with sweat.

"Have you any mental picture of the woman you are seeking?" asked Taverner.

"Nothing definite," said Black. "I only get the feel of her. But I shall know her when I see her; I am certain of that. Do you think such a woman exists? Do you think it is possible I shall ever meet her?" He appealed to us with a child's pathetic eagerness.

"Whether she is in the flesh or not I cannot say at the present moment," said Taverner, "but of her existence I have no doubt. Now tell me, when did you first notice this sensation?"

"The very first twinge I had of it," explained Black, "was as we got into the nose dive that put me to bed. We went down, down, down, faster and faster, and just as we were going to crash I *felt* something. I can't say I *saw* anything, but I got the feel of a pair of eyes. Can you realize what I mean? And when I came round from my three days' down-and-out I was in love."

"What do you dream about?" asked Taverner.

"All sorts of things; nothing especially nightmary."

"Do you notice any kind of family likeness in your dreams?"

"Now you come to mention it, I do. They all take place in brilliant sunshine. They aren't exactly Oriental, but

43

that way inclined."

Taverner laid before him a book of Egyptian travel illustrated in water-colours.

"Anything like that?" he inquired.

"My hat!" exclaimed the man. "That's the very thing." He gazed eagerly at the pictures, and then suddenly thrust the book away from him. "I can't look at them," he said; "It makes me feel—" he laid his hand on his solar plexus, hunting for a simile—"as if my tummy had dropped out."

Taverner asked our patient a few more questions, and then dismissed him with instructions to report himself if any further developments took place, saying that it was impossible to treat his trouble in its present phase. From my knowledge of Taverner's ways I knew that this meant that he required time to carry out a psychic examination of the case, which was his peculiar art, for he used his trained intuition to explore the minds of his patients as another man might use a microscope to examine the tissues of their bodies.

As it was a Friday afternoon, and Black was our last patient, I found myself free after his departure, and was walking down Harley Street wondering how I should dispose of my week-end, for an invitation I had counted upon had unexpectedly failed me. As I took a short cut through a mews lying behind the house I saw Black manoeuvring a car out of a garage. He saw me, too, and hailed me as a friend.

"You wouldn't care for a joy ride, I suppose? I am off on the trail again. Like to join me in running down the fair unknown?"

He spoke lightly, but I had had a glimpse of his soul, and knew what lay beneath. I accepted his offer, to his evident pleasure; he filled the gap left by the defection of my friends, and, moreover, I should learn more by accompanying him on one of his journeys than a dozen consulting-room examinations would tell me.

44

Never shall I forget that drive. He behaved normally till we got clear of the outlying suburbs, and then as dusk began to fall a change came over the man. At a secluded spot in the road he halted the car and stopped the engine. In the perfect stillness of that spring evening we listened to the silence. Then Black rose up in the driving-seat and uttered a peculiar cry; it was upon three minor notes, like a bird-call.

"What did you do that for?" I asked him.

"I dunno," he said; "it might attract *her* attention. You never know. It's not worth missing a chance, anyway."

He restarted the car, and I realized that the quest had begun in good earnest. I watched the needle of the speedometer creeping round the dial as we hurtled into the gathering dusk. The hedges fell away on either side of us in a grey blur. Towns and villages passed us with a roar, their inhabitants luckily keeping out of our path. Gradiants we took in our stride, and dropped into valleys like a stone from a sling. Presently from the top of a crest, we felt the Channel wind in our faces. Black hurled the car down a hill like the side of a house and pulled up dead, the bonnet nosing against promenade railings. Ahead lay the sea. Nothing else, I am convinced, could have stopped our career. Black stared at the surf for a few moments; then he shook his head.

"I have missed her again," he said, and backed the car off the pavement. "I got nearer to her to-night than I have ever done, though."

We put up for the night at an hotel, and next day Black drove me back again. I stipulated that we should get in before dusk. I had no wish to accompany him in pursuit of his dream again.

On my return I reported my experience to Taverner.

"It is an interesting case," he said, "and I think it will furnish a remarkably good instance of my reincarnation theory."

I knew Taverner's belief that the soul has lived many

lives before the present one, and that the experiences of those lives go to make up the character of to-day. When confronted by a mental state for which he could find no adequate cause in the present, it was his custom to investigate the past, getting the record of the previous lives of his patient by those secret means of which he was master. During the early days of my association with Taverner I considered these records imaginary, but when I saw how Taverner, working upon this idea, was able to foretell not only what a person would do, but in what circumstances he would find himself, I began to see that in this curious old theory of the East we might find the key to much of the baffling mystery of human life.

"You think that Black is feeling the effect of some experience in a past life?" I asked.

"Something like that," said Taverner. "I think that the spinning nose-dive had the effect of hypnotising him, and he got into that particular part of his memory where the pictures of previous lives are stored."

"I suppose he is living over again some vivid past experience," I remarked.

"I don't think it is quite that," said Taverner. "If two people feel a strong emotion, either of love or hate, for each other, it tends to link them together. If this link is renewed life after life, it becomes very strong. Black has evidently formed some such link, and is feeling the drag of it. Usually these memories lie quiet, and are only roused by the appearance of the second person. Then we see those extraordinary loves and hates which disturb the ordered state of things. Black has recovered his memories owing to being hypnotised by the nose-dive. It now remains to see how he will work out his problem."

"Supposing the woman is not upon the earth?"

"Then we shall have a singularly nasty mess," said Taverner.

"And supposing she is upon the earth?"

"We may have an equally nasty mess. These attractions

46

that come through from the past know no barriers. Black would drive that car of his through the Ten Command-ments and the British Constitution to get at her. He will go till he drops."

"Our night drive only ended at the sea wall," I said.

"Precisely. And one night it won't end there. The trouble is that Black, while he was able to feel the presence of this woman in his abnormal state, was not able to locate her. To him she seemed to come from all points of the compass at once. We shall have to move with great cau-tion, Rhodes. First we must find out whether this woman is on earth or not; then we must find out what her status is. She may be a scullery-maid or a princess; old enough to be his grandmother or not yet short-coated; it won't make any difference to Black. Moreover, she may not be free, and we can hardly launch him into the bosom of a respect-able family."

Next morning Taverner informed me that his occult methods had enabled him to locate the woman, that she was on earth, and about twenty-three years of age.

"Now we must wait," he said. "Sooner or later that tremendous desire of Black's will bring them together. I wonder whether she is conscious yet of the attraction."

A few weeks later a Mrs. Tyndall brought her daughter Elaine to consult my colleague. It seemed that the girl was developing delusions. Several times she had roused the household with the announcement that there was a man in her room. She imagined that she heard someone calling her, and used to wander about at night, taking long walks after dark, and often finding herself tired out and miles from home, reduced to finding what conveyance she could for her return.

"You do not have lapses of memory?" asked Taverner.

"Never," said the girl. "I know exactly where I am and what I am doing. I feel as if I had lost something, and couldn't rest till I had found it. I go out to look for—I don't know what. I know it is ridiculous to behave in the way I do, but the impulse is so strong I yield to it in spite of myself."

"Do you feel any fear of the presence you are conscious of in your room?"

"I did at first, it seemed so strange and uncanny, but now I feel more tantalized than anything else. It is like trying to remember a name that has slipped your memory. Do you know that feeling?"

"I should like to have your daughter under observation in my nursing home," said Taverner to the mother, and I saw by this that he did not regard the case as the commonplace type of insanity it appeared to be.

Miss Tyndall was shortly installed at the Hindhead nursing home, which was Taverner's headquarters, although he used his Harley Street room for consulting purposes. I liked the girl. She had no pretensions to striking beauty, but she had character.

For some time our patient led the life of a normal girl; then one evening she came to me.

"Dr. Rhodes," she said, "I want to take one of my night walks. Will you mind very much if I do? I shall come to no harm; I know what I am doing, but I am so restless I feel that I must move about and get out into open spaces."

I spoke to Taverner. I knew of his policy of allowing his patients to follow their whims as far as possible.

"Let her go by all means," he said. "Go with her and see what she does. We cannot let the girl wander about these moors by herself, though I don't suppose she would come to the slightest harm."

Miss Tyndall and I went out into the warm darkness of the spring night. She set the pace at a swinging, effortless stride that carried us rapidly over the heather paths. We were climbing towards the heights of Hindhead, and the ascent was trying at the pace we were making. Under the lee of a little pine wood we paused.

"Listen," said the girl, "how still it is. Do you know anything about birds? We have an owl near us at home that hoots on three notes. I have never been able to find out where he is. I often hear him shortly after dusk."

We had passed the point where the old coach road crossed the modern metalled highway. Below us was the monument to the memory of the murdered sailor, and above stood the great Celtic cross that gives rest to the souls of hanged men. Far away in the still night a car with open throttle was coming up from Thursley. We watched it as it tore past us, a shadow behind the glare of its headlights. I thought of that wild night ride to the coast, and wondered whether there was another soul in torment who sought to escape by speed from the hell within.

The girl at my side suddenly clutched my arm.

"I feel as if my soul would be torn out of my body," she gasped. "I am being drawn into a whirlpool. What is happening? What does it mean?"

I soothed her as best I could, and we set out upon the walk home. Miss Tyndall was now thoroughly overwrought, starting at every bush.

Suddenly she paused listening.

"Here it comes," she said.

Neither she nor I saw anything, but I was as certain as she was that we were not alone.

"Gipsies are numerous in these parts," I said.

"It is not gipsies," she answered, "it is the Presence. I know it quite well. There is no need to be alarmed; it never does any harm, but isn't it a curious feeling?"

She paused and looked at me, her face tense in the uncertain light that precedes moonrise. "There is something I want Dr. Rhodes; I don't know what it is, but I shall go on wanting it till I die, and never want anything else. If I do not find it, then I shall know that I have lived my life in vain."

When we returned we found that Taverner was out. An accident had occurred at the Hindhead cross-roads; the local doctors were not available, and Taverner, although he took no part in the general practice of the neighborhood, had been telephoned for to give first aid. Miss Tyndall wished me good-night and went to her room, and I was debating whether I would go to bed when the telephone bell rang.

"That you, Rhodes?" said Taverner's voice. "I am bringing a man back here. Will you have a bed made up for a surgical case?"

It was not long before I heard the car outside, and helped to unload the improvised stretcher.

"Another curious coincidence," said Taverner, with the one-sided smile he reserved for scepticism, and I saw that the man we were lifting was Arnold Black.

"Then it was his car we heard on the Portsmouth road," I cried.

"Very likely," said Taverner. "He was driving at his usual gait, failed to negotiate the cross-roads, and rolled down the bank into the bushes."

"The steering gear must have gone wrong," I said.

"Or the man's mind," said Taverner.

We got our patient into bed and were settling him down for the night, when a nurse came along to say that Miss Tyndall was in a very excited state. We left the woman in charge of Black and went along to the girl's bedroom.

We found her sitting up in bed—excited, as the nurse had said, but still mistress of herself.

"It is the Presence," she said; "it is so strong that I feel as if at any moment I might see something."

Taverner lowered the light. "Let us see if we can get a look at it," he observed.

It is a peculiarity of a mystic that his presence stimulates the psychic faculties of those he is with, and Taverner was a mystic of no ordinary type. I have nothing of the mystic in my make up, but when astral entities are about I am conscious of a sensation such as we considered in childhood to be due to a goose walking over one's grave. Taverner would often describe to me the appearance of the thing that gave rise to these sensations as it presented itself to his trained sight, and after a little practice I found that, although I was seldom able to see anything, I could locate the direction whence the vibrations came.

As we waited in the darkened room I became conscious of this sensation, and then Taverner exclaimed:

"Look, Rhodes, even you must see this, for it is the etheric double coming out of the physical body."

Beside the girl on the bed a coffin-shaped drift of grey mist was spreading itself. As we watched it I saw it take form, and I could trace the distinct outline of a human figure. Slowly the features grew clear, and I recognized the lean Red Indian countenance of Arnold Black. The girl rose on her elbow and stared in astonishment at the form beside her. Then with a cry she sought to gather the grey drift into her arms.

"It has come—it has come," she cried. "Look. I can see it. It is real." But the impalpable stuff eluded her, her hands passed through it as through a fog-wreath, and with a cry of distress she hung over the form she could not hold.

"What does it all mean?" I asked Taverner.

"It means death if we can't get it back," he said. "That is Black's etheric double, what you would call his ghost, the subtle body that carries the life forces. It is inspired by emotions, and, being freed for the time, has come to the object of its desires—the reborn soul of the woman he loved in the past. The astral body has often been here before; it was that of which she was conscious when she felt what she calls 'the Presence,' but it has never previously been able to come in such a definite form as this. It means that Black is on the point of death. We must see if we can induce this grey shape to re-enter its house of flesh."

Taverner laid his hand on the girl's shoulder, compelling her attention.

"Come with me," he said.

"I cannot leave It," she replied, again seeking to gather

51

up the shadowy form on the bed.

"It will follow you," said Taverner.

Meekly the girl rose. I put her dressing gown over her shoulders and Taverner held open the door for her. She preceded us into the passage, the grey mist-wreath drifting after her, its outlines merged in a shapeless fog. It was no longer horizontal but upright, looking like a sheet held up by the corner. The girl moved ahead of us down the passage; with her hand on the door of the room where Black lay she paused, then she entered, and started back in confusion as the light of a nightlight revealed the form of a man in the bed.

"I—I beg your pardon," she faltered, and sought to retreat, but Taverner pushed her ahead of him and closed the door.

He led her gently to the bed. "Have you ever seen this man before?" he asked.

"Never," she replied, staring with a curious fascination at the set face on the pillow.

"Look straight into yourself, face your naked soul, and tell me what he is to you."

Taverner's will compelled her, and the veneer of to-day fell away from her; the greater self that had come down through the ages stirred, woke, and for the moment took control of the lesser personality.

A man's life and the fate of two souls hung in the balance, and Taverner forced the girl to face the issue.

"Look down into your deeper self and tell me what this man is to you."

"Everything."

The girl faced him, breathing as if she had run a race.

"What will you do for him?"

"Everything."

"Think well before you pledge yourself, for if you bring that soul back into the body and then fail it, you will have committed a very grievous sin."

"I could not fail it if I tried," replied the girl. "Something stronger than myself compels me."

"Then bid the soul re-enter the body and live again."

"Is he dead?"

"Not yet, but his life hangs by a thread. Look, you can see it."

We looked, and saw that the silvery strand of mist connected the grey wraith with the body on the bed.

"How can I make him re-enter his body?"

"Focus your mind on the body and he will be attracted back into it."

Slowly, hesitatingly, she bent over the unconscious man and gathered the bruised and broken body into her arms. Then, as we watched, the grey drifting mist drew nearer and was gradually absorbed into the physical form.

Black and Elaine Tyndall were married from the nursing home six weeks later, and left for their honeymoon in the racing car that had been salved from the bushes. There was nothing wrong with the steering gear.

As we returned to the house after watching their departure I said to Taverner: "Most men would say you had mated a couple of lunatics whose delusions happened to match."

"And most men would have certified the pair of them for an asylum," replied Taverner. "All I have done has been to recognize the working of two great natural laws, and you see the result."

"How did you piece this story together?" I inquired.

"It was fairly simple," said Taverner, "as simple as human nature ever is. You know my method. I believe that we have many lives and can influence others by our thoughts, and I find that my belief will often throw light where ordinary ideas fail.

"Now take the case of Black. The ordinary doctor would have said it was his subconscious mind that was playing him tricks; well, it might have been, so I took the trouble to read the history of his past lives in what we call the Akashic Records, where all thoughts are recorded. I found that in several previous lives he had been associated with an individual of the opposite sex, and that in his last life he had had the presumption to bid for her favour when she was a princess of the Royal house and he was a soldier of fortune.

"As a reward for his daring he was flung from the roof of the palace and dashed to death on the stones of the court-yard. Now you can understand why it was that the spinning nose dive wakened old memories—he had plunged to his death before; you can also see why he felt 'as if his tummy had dropped out' when he saw the pictures of Egypt, for it was in an Egyptian existence that all this took place. There are a great many people alive at the present time who have had an Egyptian past; we seem to be running into a cycle of them.

"You can also see the reason of Black's love of speed; it waked dim memories of his last contact with the soul he was seeking. If he could retrace his steps to the point where he swooped into space he would be able to pick up the trail of the woman of his desire. He was prompted to reproduce as nearly as possible the conditions in which he had last known her.

"As I have already told you, the memories woke, and Black set forth on his quest for the woman he had been mated with life after life, and having seen in the occult records their repeated union, I knew it was only a matter of time till they came together, and I sincerely hoped that she, too, would remember the past and be free to marry him. If she had not, we should have had, as I warned you, a very nasty mess. These spiritual ties are the devil.

"Now, I expect you wonder what chance it was that brought Elaine Tyndall to me. I knew, as I told you, that sooner or later their paths would meet. Well, I placed my-self mentally at the point of their meeting; consequently as time drew near, they converged upon me, and it was my privilege to steer them to harbour."

54

"But what about Miss Tyndall and her delusions?" I inquired.

"It looked to you like a commonplace case of old maid's insanity, didn't it?" said Taverner. "But the girl's self-possession and absence of fear led me to suspect something more; she was so very definite and impersonal in her attitude towards her delusions. So I arranged for her to come down to Hindhead and let me try whether or not I could see what she saw.

"What we saw you yourself know; it was Black shaken out of his body by the shock of the accident and drawn to her by the intensity of his longing, not at all an uncommon phenomenon; I have often seen it."

"How did you manage to get Black to re-enter his body, provided he had ever been out of it?"

"When Elaine touched his body, the soul of Black realized that it could meet her in the flesh, and so sought to re-enter its own body, but the vitality was so low it could not manage it. If the girl had not held him in her arms as she did, he would have died, but he lived on her vitality till he was able to build up his own."

"I can see the psychological end of it," I said, "but how do you account for the chances that brought them together? Why should Miss Tyndall have become restless and made for the Portsmouth road, timing her arrival to fit in with Black's passing?"

Taverner looked up at the stars that were just beginning to show in the darkening sky.

"Ask Them," he said. "The ancients knew what they were about when they cast horoscopes."

The Soul That Would Not Be Born

Contrary to his usual custom, Taverner did not insist on seeing his patient alone, for the sufficient reason that no information could be extracted from her. It was to the mother, a Mrs. Cailey, we turned for the case history, and she, poor anxious woman, gave us such scanty details as an onlooker might observe; but of the viewpoint and feelings of the patient we learnt nothing, for there was nothing to learn.

She sat before us in the big leather armchair; her body was a tenement for the soul of a princess, but it was, alas, untenanted. The fine dark eyes, utterly expressionless, looked into space while we discussed her as if she had been an inanimate object, which practically she was.

"She was never like ordinary children," said the mother. "When they put her in my arms after she was born she looked up at me with the most extraordinary expression in her eyes; they were not a baby's eyes at all, Doctor, they were the eyes of a woman, and an experienced woman too. She didn't cry, she never made a sound, but she looked as if she had all the troubles of the world upon her shoulders. That baby's face was a tragedy; perhaps she knew what was coming."

"Perhaps she did," said Taverner.

"In a few hours, however," continued the mother, "she looked quite like an ordinary baby, but from that time to this she has never changed, except in her body."

We looked at the girl in the chair, and she gazed back at us with the unblinking stolidity of a very young infant.

"We have taken her to everybody we could hear of, but

56

they all say the same—that it is a hopeless case of mental deficiency; but when we heard of you, we thought you might say something different. We knew that your methods were not like those of most doctors. It does seem strange that it should be impossible to do anything for her. We passed some children playing in the street as we came here in the car—bonny, bright little things, but in such rags and dirt. Why is it that those, whose mothers can do so little for them, should be so splendid, and Mona, for whom we would do anything, should be—as she is?"

The poor woman's eyes filled with tears, and neither Taverner nor I could reply.

"I will take her down to my nursing home and keep her under observation for a time, if you wish," said Taverner. "If the brain is at fault, I can do nothing, but if it is the mind itself that has failed to develop I might attempt the cure. These deficiency cases are so inaccessible—it is like ringing up on the telephone when the subscriber will not answer. If one could attract her attention, something might be done; the crux of the matter lies in the establishment of communications."

When they had gone, I turned to Taverner and said: "What hope have you in dealing with a case like that?"

"I cannot tell you just yet," he replied; "I shall have to find out what her previous incarnations have been. I invariably find that congenital troubles originate in a former life. Then I shall have to work out her horoscope and see whether the conditions are ripe for the paying off of whatever debt she may have incurred in a previous life. Do you still think I am a queer sort of charlatan, or are you beginning to get used to my ways?"

"I have long ceased to be astonished at anything," I replied. "I should accept the devil, horns, hoofs and tail, if you undertook to prescribe for him."

Taverner chuckled.

"With regard to our present case, I am of the opinion that we shall find the law of reincarnation is the one we

57

shall have to look to. Now tell me this Rhodes—supposing reincarnation is not a fact, supposing this life is the beginning and end of our existence and at its conclusion we proceed to flames or harps according to the use we have made of it, how do you account for Mona Cailey's condition? What did she do in the few hours between her birth and the onset of her disease to bring down such a judgment on herself? And at the end of her life, can she justly be said to have deserved hell or earned Heaven?"

"I don't know," said I.

"But supposing my theory is right; then, if we can recover the record of her past, we shall be able to find the cause of her present condition, and having found the cause we may be able to remedy it. At any rate, let us try.

"Would you like to see how I recover the records? I use various methods; sometimes I get them by hypnotizing the patients or by crystal-gazing, and sometimes I read them from the subconscious mind of Nature. You know, we believe that every thought and impulse in the world is recorded in the Akashic Records. It is like consulting a reference library. I am going to use the latter method in the present case."

In a few moments, by methods known to himself, Taverner had shut out all outward impressions from his mind, and was concentrated upon the inner vision.

Confused mental pictures evidently danced before his eyes; then he got the focus and began to describe what he saw while I took down notes.

Egyptian and Grecian lives were dismissed with a few words; these were not what he sought; he was merely working his way down through the ages, but I gathered that we were dealing with a soul of ancient lineage and great opportunities. Life after life we heard the tale of royal birth or initiation into the priesthood, and yet, in its present life, the girl's soul was cut off from all communication with its physical vehicle. I wondered what abuse of opportunity had led to such a sentence of solitary confinement in the cell of its body.

Then we came to the level we sought, Italy in the fifteenth century, as it turned out. "Daughter of the reigning
duke—." I could not catch the name of his principality.
"Her younger sister was beloved by Giovanni Sigmundi;
she contrived to win the affections of her sister's lover, and
then, a richer suitor offering for her own hand, she betrayed Sigmundi to his enemies in order to be free of his
importunities."

"A true daughter of the Renaissance," said Taverner
when he had returned to normal consciousness and read
my notes, for he seldom retained any memory of what
transpired during his subconscious states. "Now I think
we can guess the cause of the trouble. I wonder whether
you are aware of the mental processes that precede birth?
Just before birth the soul sees a cinematograph film (as it
were) of its future life; not all the details, but the broad
outlines which are determined by its fate; these things it
cannot alter, but according to its reaction to them, so will
its future lives be planned. Thus it is that although we cannot alter our fate in this life, our future lies entirely in our
own hands.

"Now we know the record, we can guess what manner
of fate lies upon this girl. She owes a life debt to a man and
a woman; the suffering she caused recoils upon her. There
is no need for a specialized hell; each soul builds its own."

"But she is not suffering," I said; "she is merely in a passive condition. The only one who suffers is the mother."

"Ah," said Taverner, "therein lies the crux of the whole
matter. When she had that brief glimpse of what lay before her, she rebelled against her fate and tried to repudiate
her debt; her soul refused to take up the heavy burden. It
was this momentary flash of knowledge which gave her
eyes their strange, unchildlike look which so startled her
mother."

"Do people always have this foreknowledge?" I asked.

"They always have that glimpse, but its memory usually

59

lies dormant. Some people have vague premonitions, however, and occult training tends to recover these lost memories, together with others belonging to previous lives."

"Having found out the cause of Miss Cailey's trouble, what can you do to cure her?"

"Very little," said Taverner. "I can only wait and watch her. When the time is ripe for the settlement of the balance, the other actors in the old tragedy will come along and unconsciously claim the payment of their debt. She will be given the opportunity of making restitution and going on her way fate-free. If she is unable to fulfil it, then she will be taken out of life and rapidly forced back into it again for another attempt, but I think (since she has been brought to me) her soul is to be given another chance of entering its body. We will see."

I often used to watch Mona Cailey after she was installed at the Hindhead nursing home. In spite of its mask-like expressionlessness, her face had character. The clearly cut features, firm mouth, and fine eyes were fitting abode for a soul of no ordinary calibre—only that soul was not present.

It was Taverner's expectation that the other actors in the drama would appear upon the scene before very long, brought to the girl's vicinity by those strange currents that are for ever on the move beneath the surface of life. As each new patient arrived at the nursing home, I used to watch Mona Cailey narrowly, wondering whether the newcomer would demand of her the payment of the ancient debt that held her bound.

Spring passed into summer and nothing happened. Other cases distracted my attention, and I had almost forgotten the girl and her problems when Taverner reminded me of them.

"It is time we began to watch Miss Cailey," he said. "I have been working out her horoscope, and a conjunction of planets is taking place towards the end of the month which would provide an opportunity for the working out of her fate—if we can get her to take it."

"Supposing she does not take it?"

"Then she will not be long in going out, for she will have failed to achieve the purpose of this incarnation."

"And supposing she takes it?"

"Then she will suffer, but she will be free, and she will soon rise again to the heights she had previously gained."

"She is hardly likely to belong to a royal house in this life," I said.

"She was more than royal; she was an Initiate," replied Taverner, and from the way he said the word I knew he spoke of a royalty that is not of this earth.

Our words were suddenly interrupted by a cry from one of the upper rooms. It was a shriek of utter terror such as a soul might give that had looked into chaos and seen forbidden horrors; it was the cry of a child in nightmare, only—and this added to its ghastliness—it came from the throat of a man.

We rushed upstairs; we had no need to ask whence that cry came; there was only one case that could have uttered it—a poor fellow suffering from shell-shock whom we were keeping in bed for a rest.

We found him standing in the middle of the floor, shaking from head to foot. At sight of us he rushed across and flung himself into Taverner's arms. It was the pathetic action of a frightened child, but carried out by the tall figure in striped pyjamas, it was extraordinarily distressing to witness.

Taverner soothed him as gently as a mother, and got him back to bed, sitting by him until he quieted down.

"I do not think we will keep him in bed any longer," said my colleague after we had left the room. "The inactivity is making him brood, and he is living over again the scenes of the trenches."

Accordingly, Howson appeared among the patients next day for the first time since his arrival, and seemed to benefit by the change.

The benefit was not of long duration, however; when once the novelty had worn off, he commenced his brooding again, going over mentally the horrors he had lived through, and ending each recall with an attack of panic terror, rushing to the nearest human being for protection.

It proved somewhat distressing to our other patients to have six feet of burly humanity hurled unexpectedly into their arms, so we segregated Howson in the portion of the garden we kept for cases that we could not mix with the rest. The only other occupant of this part of the garden was Mona Cailey, but we hardly counted her, for she sat motionless in the deck chair we placed for her, never stirring until she was fetched in to meals.

As I was walking one evening with Taverner in that part of the grounds, we heard the now familiar sound of poor Howson's nightmare shriek. He shot out of the summer-house and stood irresolutely on the lawn. The only people in sight were ourselves and Mona Cailey, passive in her chair; he was about half-way between the two. When a man's nerve is broken he reverts either to the savage or the child, according to his temperament, and for the time being Howson was about four years old. Taverner hurried towards him over the intervening grass, but when a man reverts to the child, it is to the mother he turns, and, ignoring the approaching man, Howson ran across the lawn to Mona Cailey and buried his face in her lap.

The impact of the heavy man, flung upon her with utter abandonment, nearly sent the girl, chair and all, over backwards, and startled even her dim brain into some measure of response. I was about to run forward and extricate her from her embarrassing position, when Taverner caught my arm and stopped me.

"No, watch," he said. "See what she does. This may be the working out of her fate."

There was nothing offensive in Howson's behaviour, for he was so obviously a child and not a man. He always used to remind me of a mastiff that has been nursed as a puppy and cannot realize when it has ceased to be a lap-dog.

For several endless minutes we watched the dim brain trying to work, and then a hand, white and beautifully formed, but limp, as only the hands of the mentally afflicted are limp, was laid on the man's heaving shoulder. It was the first thought-out action that Mona Cailey had ever performed.

I thought Taverner would have danced upon the lawn in his delight.

"Look!" he said. "Watch her mind trying to work."

I watched. It was like nothing so much as rusty machinery being reluctantly turned over by hand. The girl's un-lined forehead was contracted with effort as the thought-currents forced their way through the unopened channels. What dim mother instincts awoke I do not know, but she had evidently taken the big child at her feet under her protection.

In a few minutes Howson recovered his self-control and made his embarrassed apologies to the victim of his on-slaught. The fine dark eyes gazed steadily back into his without a trace of expression, and realizing the state of affairs, he stopped his apologies in the middle of a sentence and stared back at her.

"Oh, well," he said, as much to himself as to her, "if you don't mind, I'm sure I'm thankful," and sitting at her feet he lit a cigarette with shaking hands.

From that time onwards the pair were inseparable during their waking hours. To Howson, the passive presence seemed to afford just the companionship he needed. She gave him a sense of human protection, and yet he did not feel that in her eyes he was making a fool of himself. This curious comradeship between the mindless girl and the alert intelligent man was a source of great amusement to other inmates of the home, and I myself was inclined to re-gard it as one of those strange friendships that spring up between the most incongruous cases in such a house as ours, until my colleague put his hand on my shoulder one evening as the two were crossing the lawn towards the house.

"Who is that with Mona Cailey?" he asked.

"Howson, of course," I replied, surprised at the obviousness of such a question.

"So we call him now," said Taverner, watching the pair closely, "but I think there was a time when he answered to the name of Giovanni Sigmundi."

"You mean—?" I exclaimed.

"Exactly," said Taverner. "The wheel has come round the full circle. When he was dying by torture in the hands of those to whom she betrayed him, he called for her in his agony. Needless to say, she did not come. Now that he is in agony again, some strange law of mental habit carried the call for help along the old channels, and she has answered it. She has begun to repay her debt. If all goes well, we may see that soul come right back into its body, and it will not be a small soul that comes into the flesh if that happens."

I had thought that we were going to witness a romance of re-united lovers, but I was soon made aware that it was more likely to be a tragedy for one at least of them.

Next day Howson's fiancee arrived to visit him. I took her out to the secluded part of the garden where he spent his time, and there saw enacted a most pathetic little tragicomedy. As usual, Howson was at Mona Cailey's side, smoking his interminable cigarettes. At sight of his fiancee he sprang to his feet; Mona Cailey also rose. In the eyes of the newcomer there were fear and distrust, perhaps occasioned by her unfamiliarity with mental cases, which are always distressing at first sight, but in the eyes of our defective there was a look which I can only describe as contempt. There was one flash of the astute ruthlessness of the fifteenth century Italian, and I guessed who the newcomer was.

Howson, forgetful of the other girl's presence, advanced

eagerly to meet his fiancee and kissed her, and I thought for a moment we were going to be treated to one of those nasty outbursts of spitefulness of which defectives are capable, when a sudden change came over Mona Cailey, and I saw that marvelous thing, a soul enter and take possession of its body.

Intelligence slowly dawned in the misty eyes as she watched the scene being enacted before her. For a moment the issue hung in the balance; would she rush forward and tear them apart, or would she stand aside? Behind the oblivious lovers I poised myself for a spring, ready to catch her if necessary. For ages we waited thus while the unpracticed brain moved reluctantly in its unaccustomed effort.

Then the girl turned away slowly. Over the grass she moved, silently, unnoticed by the other two, seeking the shelter of the shrubberies as a wounded animal seeks cover, but her movements were no longer those of unguided limbs; she moved as a woman moves who has walked before kings, but as a woman stricken to the heart.

I followed her as she passed under the trees and put my hand on her arm, instinctively speaking words of comfort, although I expected no response. She turned on me dark eyes full of unshed tears and luminous with a terrible knowledge.

"It has to be," she said distinctly, perfectly, the first words she had ever uttered. Then she withdrew her arm from my hand and went on alone.

During the days that followed we watched the soul swing in and out of the body. Sometimes we had the mindless imbecile, and sometimes we had one of those women who have made history. Save that her means of communication developed slowly, she was often in full possession of her faculties. And what faculties they were! I had read of the wonderful women of the Renaissance—now I saw one.

Then, sometimes, when the pain of her position became too great to be borne, the soul would slip out for a while and rest in some strange Elysian fields we know not of, leaving to us again the care of the mindless body. But each time it came back refreshed. Whom it had talked with, what help had been given, we never knew; but each time it faced the agony of reincarnation and took up its burden with renewed courage and knowledge.

The dim, newly-awakened mind understood Howson through and through; each twist and turn of him, conscious and subconscious, she could follow, and of course she was the most perfect nurse he could have had. The panic-striken mind was never allowed to thrash about in outer darkness and the horror of death. Instinctively she sensed the approach of nightmare forms, and putting out her hand, pulled the wandering soul back into safety.

Thus protected from the wear and tear of his terrible storms, Howson's mind began to heal. Day by day the time drew nearer when he would be fit to leave the nursing home and marry the woman he was engaged to, and day by day, by her instinctive skill and watchful care, Mona Cailey quickened the approach of that time.

I have said that he would leave and marry the woman he was engaged to—not the woman he loved—for at that time had Mona Cailey chosen to lift one finger she could have brought the old memories into consciousness and drawn Howson to herself; and that she was fully aware of this, I who watched her, am convinced. An ignorant woman could not have steered round the pitfalls as skilfully as she did.

The night before he was to leave she had a bad relapse into her old condition. Hour after hour Taverner and I sat beside her while she scarcely seemed to breathe, so completely was the soul withdrawn from the body.

"She is shut up in her own subconsciousness, moving among the memories of the past," Taverner whispered to me, as slight twitchings ran through the motionless form on the bed.

Then a change took place.

"Ah," said Taverner, "she is out now!"

Slowly the long white hand was raised—the hand that I had watched change from a limp thing of disgust to firmness and strength, and a sequence of knocks was given upon the wall at the bedside that would have skinned the knuckles of an ordinary hand.

"She is claiming entrance to her Lodge," whispered Taverner. "She will give the Word as soon as the knocks are acknowledged."

From somewhere up near the ceiling the sequence of knocks was repeated, and then Taverner placed his hand across the girl's mouth. Through the guarding fingers came some muffled sound I could not make out.

"She will get what she has gone to seek," said Taverner. "It is a high Degree to which she is claiming admission."

What transpired during the workings of that strange Lodge which meets out of the body I had no means of knowing. I could see that Taverner, however, with his telepathic faculties, was able to follow the ritual, for he joined in the responses and salutes.

As the uncanny ceremony drew to its close we saw the soul that was known to us as Mona Cailey withdraw from the company of its brethren and, plane by plane, return to normal consciousness. On her face was that look of peace which I had never before seen in the living, and only on the faces of such of the dead as went straight out into the Light.

"She has gathered strength for her ordeal," said Taverner, "and it will indeed be an ordeal, for Howson's fiancee is fetching him in her car."

"Will it be wise to let Miss Cailey be present?" I asked.

"She must go through with it," said Taverner. "It is better to break than to miss an opportunity."

He was a man who never spared his patients when there was a question of fate to be worked out. He thought less of death than most people think of emigration; in fact, he seemed to regard it in exactly that light.

"Once you have had some memory glimpse, however dim, of your own past, you are certain of your future;

therefore you cease to fear life. Supposing I make a mess of an experiment to-day, I clear up the mess, go to bed, sleep, and then, in the morning when I am rested, I start again. You do the same with your lives when once you are sure of reincarnation. It is only the man who does not realize as a personal fact the immortality of the soul who talks of a ruined life and opportunities gone never to return."

Mona Cailey, Taverner, and myself were on the doorstep to bid good-bye to Howson when his fiancee called to take him away. He thanked us both with evident feeling for what we had done for him, but Taverner waved a disclaiming hand towards the girl at his elbow.

"You have had nothing from me but board and lodging," he said. "There is your psychologist."

Howson took Mona's hand in both his. She stood absolutely passive, but not with her usual limp inertia; it was the motionlessness of extreme tension.

"Poor little Mona!" he said. "You are a lot better than you used to be. Go on getting better, and one of these days you may be a real girl and have a good time," and he kissed her lightly as one would kiss a child.

What memories that kiss awakened I cannot say, but I saw him change colour and look at her sharply. Had one glimmer of response lightened those dark eyes, the old love would have returned, but there was no change in the mask-like countenance of the woman who was paying her debt. He shivered. Perhaps some cold breath from the torturers' dungeon touched him. He got into the car beside the woman he was to marry, and she drove away.

"How will that marriage turn out?" I asked as the sounds of the car died in the distance.

"Like a good many others where only the emotions are mated. They will be in love for a year, then will come dis-illusionment, and after they have bumped through the crisis, held together by the pressure of social opinion, they will settle down to the mutual toleration which passes for a successful marriage. *But when he comes to die, he will remember this Mona Cailey and call for her, and as he crosses the threshold she will claim him, for they have made restitution, and the way is clear."*

The Scented Poppies

I

"Mr. Gregory Polson," said Taverner, reading the card that had been brought to him. "Evidently a junior member of the firm. Lincoln's Inn is where they have their abode, so they are probably solicitors. Let us have a look at him."

A man's work generally puts its mark on him, and our visitor, although a comparatively young man, already showed the stamp of the legal profession.

"I want to consult you," he began, "about a very curious matter—I cannot call it a case. It seems to me, however, that you are the only man who can deal with it and therefore—although it may not be strictly in your line—I should be exceedingly grateful to you if you would look into it."

Taverner nodded his acquiescence, and our visitor took up the burden of his story.

"I daresay you have heard of old Benjamin Burmister, who made such an enormous fortune during the War? We—that is, my father's firm—are his solicitors and are also personal friends of the family, or, to be exact, his brothers' families, for old Mr. Burmister is unmarried. My sister and I have grown up with the two sets of Burmister cousins as if we were all one big household; in fact, my sister is at present engaged to one of David Burmister's boys—an awfully nice chap, my particular friend, in fact. We are very pleased about the engagement, for the Burmisters are nice people, although the other two brothers were not wealthy. Well, to make a long story short, after Edith and Tim had been engaged about six months, my people were a lot more pleased about the engagement (but I can't say that I am, however), for old Benjamin Burmister

70

made a new will leaving his money to Tim."

"Why should you regard this as a disadvantage?"

"Because the people he has left his money to have an unfortunate knack of committing suicide."

"Indeed?"

"Yes," said our visitor, "it has happened upon no fewer than three occasions. The will I have just completed in favour of Tim is his fourth. Murray, Tim's eldest brother, who was the last one Mr. Burmister had chosen to be his heir, jumped off a cliff near Brighton about a month ago."

"You say that each time Mr. Burmister makes a will, the principal beneficiary commits suicide?" said Taverner. "Can you tell me the conditions of the will?"

"They are rather unfair in my opinion," said Gregory Polson. "Instead of dividing the money among his nephews and nieces, who are none too well off, he insists upon leaving the bulk of it to one nephew. His idea seems to be that he will found a kind of dynasty—he has already purchased the country seat—and that he will make one Burmister an influential man, instead of making about a dozen of them comfortable."

"I see," said Taverner, "and as soon as the will is made the principal beneficiary commits suicide."

"That is it," said Polson; "they have had three suicides in two years."

"Tut, tut," said Taverner, "as many as that? It certainly does not look like chance. Now who has benefited by these deaths?"

"Only the next heir, who speedily commits suicide himself."

"What determines your client in his choice of an heir?"

"He picks the nephew whom he thinks is most likely to do him credit."

"He does not follow any rule of birth?"

"None whatever. He chooses according to his estimate of their character, picking the more forceful natures first. Tim is a much quieter, more retiring kind of fellow than his

71

cousins—I was rather surprised to see old Burmister's selection fall on him—but there is not much choice now;there are only three boys left after these ghastly tragedies."

"Then it is one of these three men who will ultimately benefit if another suicide takes place?"

"That is so. But one can hardly conceive a criminal cold blooded enough to kill off an entire family on the off-chance that the final choice might fall upon himself!"

"What manner of men are these three remaining cousins?"

"Henry is an engineer, doing quite well and engaged to be married. He will never set the Thames on fire, but he is a decent chap. He is Tim's younger brother. Bob, Tim's cousin, is a bit of a ne'er-do-well. We have had to extricate him from a breach of promise and one or two other unpleasantnesses, but I should say he was a good-hearted, irresponsible lad, his own worst enemy. The last of the family is Irving, Bob's brother, a harmless enough chap, but not fond of honest work. Joseph Burmister's boys never did as well as David's; they inclined to the artistic rather than the practical, and that type never makes money.

"Joseph's wife, however, had a fair amount, and each of her children has about a hundred and fifty a year of his own; not affluence, but it keeps them out of the work-house. Bob does odds and ends to supplement his means; he is secretary of a Golf Club at present, but Irving is the family genius and has set out to be an artist, though I don't think he has ever produced anything. His sole occupation, so far as I know, is to write a monthly art criticism for a paper that thinks publicity is sufficient payment."

"He will not get very fat at that rate," said Taverner. "How does he manage to exist on his hundred and fifty?"

"He lives in a single room studio and eats out of a frying pan. It is not so unattractive as it sounds, however; he has extraordinarily good taste, and has got his little place quite charming."

"So these are the people who might possibly benefit under the will—a steady-going engineer, a good-natured scatterbrain, and an artistic Bohemian."

"There were originally seven possible beneficiaries, providing old Benjamin adhered to his policy. Three are dead by their own hand, one is at present under sentence of death—"

"What do you mean by that?" interrupted Taverner quickly.

"Ah!" said Polson, "that is the thing that gave me a nasty turn, and made me come to you. The three men who are dead all committed suicide in the same way by flinging themselves from a height. Tim was in my office yesterday; our chambers are at the top of the building, a considerable height up. He leant out of the window for quite a while, and when I asked him what he was looking at he said: 'I wonder what it would feel like to take a header on to the pavement.' I told him to come in and not play the fool but it gave me a nasty shock, coming on top of the other suicides, so I came to you."

"Why to me?" asked Taverner.

"I have read something of occultism and something of psychology and heard how you work the two systems in combination," said Polson, "and it seemed to me that this was a case for you."

"There is more in this than you have told me," said Taverner. "What is it that you suspect?"

"I have no evidence whatever; in fact, it is the lack of evidence that has made me seek an explanation outside the normal. Why should these men, perfectly healthy average individuals, take their own lives for no reason whatsoever? One cannot account for it on any of the accepted theories, but if one admits the feasibility of thought transference, and pretty nearly everybody does nowadays, then it seems to me that it would be possible to give mental suggestion to these men to commit suicide."

"It is not only possible," said Taverner, "but in less extreme forms this exercise of secret pressure is exceedingly common. I could tell you some curious stories in connection with the Great War in this line. Not all the men who were 'got at' were reached through their pockets; many were approached by the channel of their subconscious minds. But continue. There is someone whom you are watching, subconsciously, if not consciously?"

"I have given you all the facts that could possibly be admitted as evidence. I haven't got a clue that would hang a cat, but I suspect Irving."

"On what grounds?"

"On none whatever; chiefly on the principle of 'I do not like you, Dr. Fell.' "

"Give me your unbowdlerised impressions of him."

"He is not straight, sir. I have never once caught him out, but I should never trust him. Then he is in with a set I don't like the look of: they play about with hashish and cocaine and each other's wives. They are not wholesome. I prefer Bob's wild-cat company promoters to Irving's long-haired soul-mates.

"Thirdly, Irving is the last one old Benjamin would be likely to leave his money to. I think he would leave it to Irving before he left it outside the family, for he is terribly proud of the Burmister name, but he is not at all fond of the fellow. They never got on together; Benjamin is a rough, downright old chap, and Irving is a bit of an old maid. Fourthly, if you knew Bob and Henry, you would know that it was out of the question that they should do such a thing, but Irving might—when a man fools with drugs he may do anything. Besides, he has read along the same lines as I have; in fact it was he who first put me on to them."

"Have you any reason to believe that Irving is a trained occultist?"

"He is interested in occultism, but I should not imagine that he would ever train in anything; he is nothing but a dabbler."

"Then he is not very likely to be able to perform a mental assassination. Thought transference requires more effort than swinging a sledge hammer. If you are ever offered your choice between being an occultist and a blacksmith, choose the lighter job and enter the forge rather than the Lodge.

"Well, you suspect Irving? As you say, there is no evidence to hang a cat, but we will put him through the sieve and see what he yields. Did he become very intimate with old Mr. Burmister's heirs after the wills became known?"

"No more so than usual; they are a united family and always saw a lot of each other. The only thing that Irving ever did that was out of the ordinary was to decorate their rooms for them—he has a wonderful taste in colouring—but then he did that for a good many of us, and designed the girl's dresses, too. He is an extraordinary chap, who makes a hobby of that sort of thing; he knows all the out-of-the-way shops where you can get queer brands of coffee and cigarettes, and restaurants where you can get weird food. It has always seemed to me the sort of thing for a woman rather than a man to be interested in."

"Ah!" said Taverner, "he designed their rooms. Now that is a peculiarly intimate thing to do—the man who designs the place you live in can exercise a great influence over your life if he knows how to make use of his opportunities. But before we go any further afield, try and think if there was anything of any sort that the dead men had in common and the living ones have not got, any mode of life, possession, peculiarity—anything in fact, that differentiated them."

Polson racked his brains for several minutes.

"The only thing I can possibly think of," he said at length, "is a particular kind of scent that Irving manages to get hold of and gives to his particular friends. He makes a great mystery of it, but then he loves making mysteries about nothing in particular; it makes him feel important."

"Come now," said Taverner, "we have struck a warm

trail at last. The psychological effect of scents is very great; what has our friend been playing at with his mysterious smells?"

"*I* don't know," said Polson; "he probably gets it at the Stores. He had some wonderful tea once that was supposed to come direct from Lhassa, and we found a Lyons' label round it. He is that sort of chap."

"But what about this scent? Did he give it to each of the dead men and to none other?"

"He used to give it to his particular pals as a special favour. His great wheeze was to get those big poppy heads the chemists sell for making poultices, paint them all sorts of Futurist colours, stuff them with pot-pourri and fix them on the end of strips of pliable cane. They really look very well in a vase, like great gaudy flowers. He gave me a bunch once, but I wasn't honoured with the sacred perfume that he has in his own quarters; but Percy (one of the boys who was dead) had some, and he has given Tim a bunch. I am not sure whether they are scented or not."

"Then the best thing you can do is to go round to your cousin, get hold of those poppy heads, and bring them to me to have a look at."

Polson sallied forth on his mission, and as the door closed behind him, Taverner turned to me.

"You see," he said, "the advantage of intuition. Polson had nothing whatever to go on, but he instinctively distrusted Irving; when he begins to suspect foul play, he proceeds to countercheck his intuitions by observation, which is a peculiarly effective method of work, for you will see how the use of the intuition is able to point out a profitable line of observation and, by means of the subtlest and most elusive of subjective clues, lead us to what promises to be solid ground. We must see what evidence the poppy heads yield, however, before we begin to theorize. There is nothing so misleading as a preconceived opinion; one is very apt to twist the facts to fit it."

We went on to other cases, and had got to the end of our

76

appointments when the butler informed us that Mr. Polson had returned and would like to see us again. He was ushered in, bearing a long parcel in his hand, his eyes bright with excitement.

"Tim *has* been given the special scent," he cried as soon as he was inside the door.

"How did you manage to obtain possession of the poppy heads? Did you tell him why you wanted them?"

"I told him I wanted to show them to a friend. It was no use worrying him until we have something definite to go on, or he might commit suicide by sheer auto-suggestion."

"Wise man!" said Taverner. "You have read to some purpose."

Polson unrolled his parcel, and laid half-a-dozen gorgeously-colored poppy heads on the desk. They looked like wonderful tropical fruit, and certainly formed an acceptable present. Taverner examined them one by one. Five of them yielded nothing to his probing save a shower of fine black seeds, but the sixth exhaled a curious heavy perfume, and rattled when shaken.

"This poppy head," said Taverner, "is going to meet with an accident," and he crashed a paper weight down on it. Out on the blotter rolled three or four objects that looked like dried raisins, and most curious of all—a fair-sized moonstone.

At the sight of this we exclaimed as one man. Why should anyone place a gem worth several pounds in the inside of a poppyhead where it was never likely to be seen? Taverner turned over the black objects with his pencil. "Scented seeds of some sort," he remarked and handed them to me. "Smell them, Rhodes."

I took them in my hand and sniffed them gingerly.

"Not bad," I said, "but they are slightly irritating to the mucous membrane; they make me feel as if I were going to sneeze, only instead of the sneeze coming to anything, the irritation seems to run up into my head and cause a peculiar sensation as if a draught of cold air was blowing on my forehead."

"So they stir up the pineal gland, do they?" said Taverner. "I think I can see some method in the gentleman's madness. Now take the moonstone in your other hand, go on sniffing the seeds, look at the moonstone, and tell me the thoughts that come into your head, just as if you were being psycho-analysed."

I did as I was instructed.

"I think of soapy water," I began. "I think my hands would be improved by a wash. I think of a necklace of my mother's. I think this stone would be very hard to find if I dropped it out of the window. I wonder what it would be like to be thrown out of the window. I wonder what it would feel like to be thrown from a height? Does one—?"

"That will do," said Taverner, and took the moonstone away from me. I looked up in surprise, and saw that Polson had buried his face in his hands.

"My God!" he said. "And I used to play with that boy!"

I looked from one to the other of my companions in surprise.

"What does it all mean?" I asked.

"It means this," said Taverner. "Someone has hit upon a singularly ingenious way of bottling psychism. A man who is incapable, by reason of his lack of development, of doing mental work on his own account, has found a way of buying occultism by the ounce. There must be a factory where they are turning out this precious product, and where an unscrupulous scoundrel like Irving can go and buy two-penn'orth and bring it away in a paper bag."

I had always understood that occult work could only be done by men of unusual natural gifts who had devoted long years to their development, and this idea of taking your turn at the counter and buying the hidden powers like acid drops tickled my fancy. It was only the expression on Polson's face that prevented me from bursting out laughing. But I saw what deadly possibilities were latent in the plan that Taverner had outlined so grotesquely.

"There is nothing original in this scheme," said Taverner. "It is simply the commercial application of certain natural laws that are known to occultists. I have always told you that there is nothing supernatural about occult science; it is merely a branch of knowledge that has not been generally taken up, and which has this peculiarity, that its professors do not hasten to publish their results. This exceedingly clever trick of the moonstone and the scented seeds is simply an application of certain occult knowledge for the purpose of crime."

"Do you mean," said Polson, "that there is some sort of mental poison inside that poppy head? I can understand that the smell of those seeds might affect the brain, but what part does the moonstone play?"

"The moonstone is tuned to a keynote, and that keynote is suicide," said Taverner. "Someone—not Irving, he hasn't got the brains—has made a very clear mental picture of committing suicide by flinging oneself from a height, and has impressed that picture (I won't tell you how) on that moonstone, so that anyone who is in close contact with it finds the same image rise into his mind, just as a depressed person can infect others with depression without speaking one single word to them."

"But how can an inanimate object be capable of feeling emotion?" I inquired.

"It couldn't," said Taverner, "but is there such a thing as an inanimate object? Occult science teaches that there is not. It is one of our maxims that mind is entranced in the mineral, sleeps in the plant, dreams in the animal and wakes in the man. You have only to watch a sweet-pea tendril reach out for a support to realize that the movements of plants are anything but purposeless, and the work connected with the fatigue of metals is well known. Ask your barber if his razors ever get tired, and he will tell you that he rests them regularly, because fatigued steel will not take a fine edge."

"Granted," I said. "But do you mean to tell me that there is sufficient consciousness in that bit of stone to be capable of taking in an idea and transmitting it to someone's subconscious mind?"

"I do," said Taverner. "A crystal is the highest development of the mineral kingdom, and there is quite enough mind in that stone on the table to take on a certain amount of character if a sufficiently strong influence be brought to bear upon it. Remember the history of the Hope diamond and various other well-known gems whose records are known to collectors. It is this mental development of crystals which is taken advantage of in the making of talismans and amulets for which the precious stones, and next to them the precious metals, have been used from time immemorial. This moonstone is simply an amulet of evil."

"Taverner," I said, "you don't mean to tell me that you believe in charms?"

"Certainly! Don't you?"

"Good Heavens, no, not in this enlightened age!"

"My dear boy, if you find a belief universally held throughout all ages by races that have had no communication with each other, then you may be sure that there is something in it."

"Then to put it crudely," said Polson, who had hitherto stared at Taverner in silence, "you believe that someone has taught this moonstone how to give hypnotic suggestion?"

"Crudely, yes," replied Taverner, "just as middle C struck on a piano will cause the C string of another piano to vibrate in sympathy."

"How does the moonstone manage the hypnosis?" I inquired, not without malice, I am afraid.

"Ah, it has to have help with that," said Taverner. "That is where those scented seeds come in, and a more diabolically ingenious device it would be hard to find.

"Everybody is not psychic, so some means had to be devised of inducing at least temporary sensitiveness in the stolid, matter-of-fact Burmisters against whom this device was directed. As even you will admit, Rhodes, there are certain drugs that are capable of changing the condition and state of consciousness—alcohol for one, chloroform for another.

"In the East, where they know a great deal more about these things than we do, a careful study has been made of the drugs that will induce the change, and they are acquainted with many substances which the British Pharmacopoedia knows nothing about. There is a considerable number of drugs which are capable of producing, at least temporarily, a state of clairvoyance, and those black seeds are among the number. I don't know what they are—they are unfamiliar to me—but I shall try and find out, as they cannot be common, and we may then be able to trace their origin and get this devil's workshop shut down."

"Then," said Polson, "you think someone has imprinted an idea on the soul of that moonstone so that anyone who was sensitive would be influenced by it, and then added the seeds to his fiendish pot-pourri so as to drug an ordinary person into abnormal sensitiveness and make him susceptible to the influences of the moonstone?"

"Exactly!"

"And some devil manufactures these things and then sells them to dangerous fools like Irving?"

"That is my opinion."

"Then he ought to be hanged!"

"I disagree with you."

"You would let such a cold-blooded brute go unpunished?"

"No, I would not, but I would make the punishment fit the crime. Occult offences are always dealt with by occult means. There are more ways of killing a cat than drowning it in cream."

81

II

"It has not taken you long to dispose of that case," I remarked to Taverner as Polson withdrew, profuse in his thanks.

"If you think that is the end," said my colleague, "you are very much mistaken; Irving will certainly have another try, and equally certainly, I shall not let the matter rest."

"You will only get abused if you go to the police station," I told him. "If you think that twelve British grocers in a jury box would hang Irving you are very much mistaken; they would probably ask the court missionary to visit you and see if he couldn't get your family to do something for you."

"I know all that," said Taverner. "It is quite useless to go to law in a case of occult attack, but there is such a thing as the psychic police, you know. The members of all regularly organized Lodges are bound by their oath either to take up themselves or report to their fraternity any case of mental malpractice that comes within their knowledge, and we have our own way of doing justice."

"Do you intend to give Irving a dose of counter-suggestion?"

"No, I won't do that. We are not absolutely certain that he is guilty, though it looks suspiciously like it. I shall deal with him by another method, which, if he is innocent, will leave him scatheless, and if he is guilty will be singularly appropriate to his crime. The first thing, however, is to get in touch with our man without arousing his suspicions. How would you go to work, Rhodes?"

"Get Polson to introduce me," I said.

"Polson and Irving are not on any too good terms; moreover, I have the misfortune to have a certain amount of fame, and Irving will smell a rat the minute I appear in the case. Try again."

I hazarded several suggestions, from giving him a commission to paint poppyheads to falling in a fit at his feet as he issued from his studio. All of these Taverner vetoed as leaving too much to chance and likely to rouse his suspicions and prevent the possibility of a second attempt to corner him if the first failed.

"You must work along the line of his interests, and then he will fall into your hand like a ripe pear. What is the use of reading psychology if you never use it? I will bet you that before a week is out I shall have Irving begging me, as an enormous favour, to execute justice on him."

"How do you propose to go to work?" I asked.

Taverner rolled the seeds over thoughtfully with a pencil. "These things cannot be too common; I will find out first what they are and where he got them. Come along with me to Bond Street; there is a man in a perfumer's there who will probably be able to tell me what I want to know."

We were not long in arriving at our destination, and then I saw that curious little by-play that I had often witnessed when Taverner was in need of assistance. A man in a dirty white laboratory coat, who obviously did not know Taverner from Adam, was summoned from the back of the shop, my companion made a sign with his left hand that would have passed unobserved if one had not known what to look for, and immediately the attitude of our new acquaintance changed. We were led behind the counter into a room that was half laboratory, half store room, and there, amid a litter of chemical appliances, gaudy wrappers, hampers of herbs smelling up to high heaven, and the remains of a meal, the mysterious seeds were spread out for investigation.

"It is one of the Dipteryx," said the man in the white coat, "the same family as the Tonquin Bean; Dipteryx Irritans is its name. It is sometimes used for adulterating the true Tonquin bean when imported in powder form. Of course a small amount cannot be detected by any chemical tests, but you would not care to have a sachet of it among your handerchiefs; it would give you a form of hay fever, and affect your eyesight."

"Is it imported into this country much?"

"Never, save as an adulterant, and then only in powder form. It has no commercial value—you could not buy it here if you tried, in fact you could not buy it in Madagascar (where it comes from), because no scent merchant would own to having any on his premises. You would have to collect it yourself from the wild vines."

"What trade paper do you scent-makers affect?"

"We have not got one of our own, but you could get at the scent trade through the druggists' journals."

Taverner thanked him for his information, and we returned to Harley Street, where Taverner busied himself in drawing up an advertisement to the effect that a Mr. Trotter had a parcel of Dipteryx Irritans to dispose of and solicited offers.

About a week later we received, *via* the journal's office, a letter to say that a Mr. Minski, of Chelsea, was prepared to do business with us if we would furnish him with a sample and state our lowest price. Taverner chuckled when he received this epistle.

"The fish bites, Rhodes," he said. "We will proceed to call upon Mr. Minski forthwith."

I nodded my acquiescence and reached for my hat.

"Not in these clothes, Rhodes," said my colleague. "Mr. Minski would put up the shutters if he saw a top hat approaching. Let me see what I can find in my vanity bag."

His "vanity bag" was the name by which Taverner designated an old suit case that held certain disreputable garments that served him as disguise when he did not wish to obtrude his Harley Street personality upon an unappreciative world. In a few minutes I was denuded of my usual panoply, and was invested in a seedy brown suit of pseudo-smart cut; black boots that had once been brown, and a Trilby hat completed my discomfort, and Taverner, resplendent in a greenish frock coat and moth-eaten top hat, informed me that if it were not for my ruby tie-pin (which came out of a cracker) he would not altogether care to be seen out with me!

We took a bus to Victoria Station, and thence, *via* the King's Road, to our destination in an obscure side street. Mr. Minski's shop proved to be something of a surprise— we had thought to interview a man of the "old clo" dealer type, but we found that the shop we sought had some pretensions. A collection of Ruskin pottery and Futurist draperies graced the window, studio-made jewellery of the semiprecious persuasion hung in a case by the door, and Mr. Minski, in a brown velvet coat and tie like a miniature sash, made Taverner look as if he had called for the washing!

My colleague placed a forefinger, carefully begrimed at the consulting room grate, upon the velveteen coat of the owner of the shop. "You are the gentleman who wants to buy the Tonquin beans?" he inquired.

"I don't want any Tonquin beans, my good man," said that worthy impatiently. "I understood your advertisement to say that you had a parcel of Dipteryx Irritans to dispose of. The Tonquin bean belongs to a different genus, Dipteryx Odorata. I can get that anywhere, but if you are able to obtain the Irritans bean for me, we may be able to do business."

Taverner closed one eye in a revolting wink. "You know what you are talking about, young fellow," he informed the velveteen individual. "Now, are you buyin' these beans for yourself, or on commish?"

"What has that got to do with you?" demanded Mr. Minski haughtily.

"Oh, nothing," said Taverner, looking more rag-and-bony than ever, "only I prefer to do business with principals, and I always give ten per cent for introduction."

Minski opened his eyes at this, and I saw that what Taverner had guessed was probably true—Minski was buying on behalf of someone else, who might or might not be Irving. I also saw that he would not be above accepting a commission from both parties to the transaction. He had evidently been bidden to conceal the identity of his client, however, and was wondering how far he dared exceed his instructions. Finally he said: "Since you refuse to deal with me, I will communicate with my customer and see whether he is prepared to buy from you direct. Come back on Wednesday at the same time, and I will let you know."

We returned to civilization and put off the garments of our humiliation until the appointed time came round, when, dressed once more in the uniform of the shabby genteel, we returned to the shop of Mr. Minski. As we entered, we saw a man seated on a kind of divan in the corner, smoking a scented cigarette. He was, I should say, thirty-one or two years of age, sallow and unwholesome of complexion, with the pupils of his eyes unnaturally dilated; the way in which he lay back among the cushions showed that his vitality was low, and the slight tremor of the nicotine-stained fingers pointed to the cause.

Taverner, even in his shabby garments, was an imposing figure, and the man on the divan stared at him in astonishment. "You wish to purchase the Irritans variety of the Tonquin bean?" said my companion.

The man nodded, without removing the cigarette from his lips, continuing to stare at Taverner, who was adopting quite a different tone towards him from that which he had used towards Minski.

"The Irritans bean is not generally used in commerce," Taverner went on. "May I inquire for what purpose you require it?"

"That is no concern of yours," replied the man with the cigarette.

"I ask your pardon," said Taverner, "but this bean possesses certain properties not generally known outside the East, where it is raised at its true value, and I wondered whether you wished to avail yourself of these properties, for some of the beans which I hold were prepared with that end in view."

"I should very much like to!" The unnaturally bright eyes became even brighter with the speaker's eagerness.

"Are you by any chance one of *us?*" Taverner dropped his voice to a conspirator's whisper.

The bright eyes glowed like lamps. "I am exceedingly interested in these matters."

"They are subjects worthy of interest," said Taverner; "but this is a child's way of development." And he carelessly opened his hand, showing the black seeds which had come from the poppy, which served him as his pretended sample.

The cigarette came out of the languid mouth now. "Do you mean that you know something about Kundalini?"

"The Sacred Serpent Fire?" said Taverner. "Of course I am acquainted with its properties, but I do not make use of it personally. I regard its action as too drastic; it is apt to unhinge the mind that is not prepared for it. I always use the ritual method myself."

"Do you—er—undertake the training of students?" cried our new acquaintance, nearly beside himself with eagerness.

"I do occasionally, if I find a suitable type," said Taverner, absent-mindedly playing catch with the black seeds.

"I am exceedingly interested in this matter," said the man on the divan. "Would you consider me a suitable type? I am certain that I am psychic. I often see the most peculiar things."

Taverner considered him for a long moment, while he hung upon the verdict.

"It would be a small matter to put you in possession of astral vision."

Our new acquaintance sprang to his feet. "Come round to my studio," he cried; "we can talk things over quietly there. You have, I presume, a fee? I am not a rich man, but the labourer is worthy of his hire, and I would be quite willing to remunerate you for your trouble."

"My fee is five guineas," said Taverner, with an expression worthy of Uriah Heep.

The man with the scented cigarette gave a little gasp of relief; I am sure that if Taverner had added on a nought he would have paid it. We adjourned to his studio—a large, well-lit room decorated with a most bizarre mixture of colours. A couch, which probably served as a bed by night, stood at an angle in front of the fireplace; from the far corner of the room issued that indescribable odour which cannot be avoided where food is stored—a blend of bacon rind and coffee floated towards us, and the drip of some hidden tap proclaimed our host's washing accommodation.

Taverner bade him lie down on the couch, and producing a packet of dark powder from his pocket, shook some grains into a brass incense burner which stood on the mantelpiece. The heavy fumes drifted across the studio, overwhelming the domestic odours from the corner, and made me think of joss-houses and the strange rituals that propitiated hideous gods.

Except for the incense, Taverner was proceeding as in ordinary hypnotic treatment, a process with which my medical experience had rendered me familiar, and I watched the man on the couch pass rapidly into a state of deep hypnosis, and thence into a relaxed condition with almost complete cessation of the vital functions, a level to which very few hypnotists either can or dare reduce a subject. Then Taverner set to work upon one of the great centres of the body where a network of nerves converge. What his method was I could not clearly see, for his back was towards me, but it did not take many minutes, and then, with a series of swift hypnotic passes, he drew his victim back to normal consciousness.

Half dazed, the man sat up on the couch, blinking stupidly at the light; the whole process had occupied some twenty minutes, and he showed pretty plainly that he did not consider he had had his money's worth, counting out the notes to Taverner without any too good a grace.

Taverner, however, showed no disposition to go, lingering in talk, and as I noticed, watching his man closely. The latter seemed fidgety and, as we made no move, he finally said: "Excuse me, I believe there is someone at the door," and crossing the studio, quickly opened it and looked outside. Nothing but an empty passage rewarded his gaze. He returned and renewed his conversation with Taverner, but with a divided attention, from time to time glancing over his shoulder uneasily.

Then suddenly interrupting my colleague in the middle of a sentence, he said: "I am certain there is someone in the room; I have a most peculiar feeling, as if I were being watched," and he whipped aside a heavy curtain that hung across an alcove—but there was nothing but brooms and brushes behind it. Across he went to the other corner and opened a cupboard, then looked under the bed and proceeded to a systematic search of the whole studio, looking into hiding places that could barely have concealed a child. Finally, he returned to us, whose presence he seemed to have forgotten, so absorbed was he in his search.

"It is most peculiar," he said. "But I cannot get away from the feeling that I am being watched, as if some evil presence were lurking in the room waiting for my back to be turned."

Suddenly he looked upward. "What are those extraordinary balls of light moving about the ceiling?" he exclaimed.

Taverner plucked me by the sleeve. "Come along," he said, "it is time for us to be going. Irving's little friends won't be pleasant company."

We left him stock still in the centre of the room, following with his eyes the invisible object that was slowly working its way down the wall. What would happen when it reached the floor I did not inquire.

Out in the street I heaved a sigh of relief. There was something about that studio which was distinctly unpleasant. "What in the world have you done to the man?" I asked my companion.

"What I agreed to do—give him clairvoyance," replied Taverner.

"How is that going to punish him for the atrocities he has committed?"

"We don't know that he has committed any atrocities," said Taverner blandly.

"Then what are you driving at?"

"Just this. When a man gets the Sight, one of the first things he sees is his naked soul, and if that man was the one we think he is, it will probably be the last, for the soul that perpetrated those cold-blooded murders will not bear looking at. If, on the other hand, he is just an ordinary individual, neither strikingly good nor bad, then he will be the richer for an interesting experience."

Suddenly from somewhere over our heads, a blood-curdling yell rang out into the gathering dusk. It had that quality of terror which infects with panic all those who hear it, for other passers-by as well as ourselves stopped dead at the sound. A door slammed somewhere in the great echoing building we had just vacated, and then running footsteps passed rapidly down the road in the direction of the river.

"Good Lord!" I said, "he will go over the Embankment," and was startled into pursuit when Taverner laid a restraining hand on my arm.

"That is his affair, not ours," he said. "And any way, I doubt if he will face death when it comes to the point; death can be singularly nasty, you know."

He was right, for the running footsteps returned down the street, and the man we had just left passed us, flying blindly towards the flaring lights and human herd of the roaring Fulham Road.

"What is it he saw?" I demanded of Taverner, cold shivers chasing each other down my spine. I am not easily scared by anything I can see, but I frankly admit I fear the thing I cannot.

"He has met the Guardian of the Threshold," said Taverner, and his mouth snapped shut. But I had no wish to press the inquiry further; I had seen Irving's face as he passed us, and it told me all I needed to know of the nature of that strange Dweller in outer darkness.

Taverner paused to push the wad of notes in his hand into the collecting box of the Cancer Hospital.

"Rhodes," he said, "would you prefer to die and be done with, or to spend all your life in fear of death?"

"I would sooner die ten times over," I replied.

"So would I," said Taverner. "A life sentence is worse than a death sentence."

The Death Hound

"Well?" said my patient when I had finished stethoscoping him, "have I got to go softly all the days of my life?"

"Your heart is not all it might be," I replied, "but with care it ought to last as long as you want it. You must avoid all undue exertion, however."

The man made a curious grimace. "Supposing exertion seeks me out?" he asked.

"You must so regulate your life as to reduce the possibility to a minimum."

Taverner's voice came from the other side of the room. "If you have finished with his body, Rhodes, I will make a start on his mind."

"I have a notion," said our patient, "that the two are rather intimately connected. You say I must keep my body quiet,"—he looked at me—"but what am I to do if my mind deliberately gives it shocks?" and he turned to my colleague.

"That is where I come in," said Taverner. "My friend has told you what to do; now I will show you how to do it. Come and tell me your symptoms."

"Delusions," said the stranger as he buttoned his shirt. "A black dog of ferocious aspect who pops out of dark corners and chivvies me, or tries to. I haven't done him the honour to run away from him yet; I daren't, my heart's too dickey, but one of these days I am afraid I may, and then I shall probably drop dead."

Taverner raised his eyes to me in a silent question. I nodded; it was quite a likely thing to happen if the man ran far or fast.

"What sort of a beast is your dog?" enquired my colleague.

"No particular breed at all. Just plain dog, with four legs and a tail, about the size of a mastiff, but not of the mastiff build."

"How does he make his appearance?"

"Difficult to say; he does not seem to follow any fixed rule, but usually after dusk. If I am out after sundown, I may look over my shoulder and see him padding along behind me, or if I am sitting in my room between daylight fading and lamp lighting, I may see him crouching behind the furniture watching his opportunity."

"His opportunity for what?"

"To spring at my throat."

"Why does he not take you unawares?"

"This is what I cannot make out. He seems to miss so many chances, for he always waits to attack until I am aware of his presence."

"What does he do then?"

"As soon as I turn and face him, he begins to close in on me! If I am out walking, he quickens his pace so as to overtake me, and if I am indoors he sets to work to stalk me round the furniture. I tell you, he may only be a product of my imagination, but he is an uncanny sight to watch."

The speaker paused and wiped away the sweat that had gathered on his forehead during this recital.

Such a haunting is not a pleasant form of obsession for any man to be afflicted with, but for one with a heart like our patient's it was peculiarly dangerous.

"What defence do you offer to this creature?" asked Taverner.

"I keep on saying to it 'You're not real, you know, you are only a beastly nightmare, and I'm not going to let myself be taken in by you.' "

"As good a defence as any," said Taverner. "But I notice you talk to it as if it were real."

"By Jove, so I do!" said our visitor thoughtfully; "that is something new. I never used to do that. I took it for granted that the beast wasn't real, was only a phantom of my own brain, but recently a doubt has begun to creep in. Supposing the thing *is* real after all? Supposing it really has power to attack me? I have an underlying suspicion that my hound may not be altogether harmless after all."

"He will certainly be exceedingly dangerous to you if you lose your nerve and run away from him. So long as you keep your head, I do not think he will do you any harm."

"Precisely. But there is a point beyond which one may not keep one's head. Supposing, night after night, just as you were going off to sleep, you wake up knowing the creature is in the room, you see his snout coming round the corner of the curtain, and you pull yourself together and get rid of him and settle down again. Then just as you are getting drowsy, you take a last look round to make sure that all is safe, and you see something dark moving between you and the dying glow of the fire. You daren't go to sleep, and you can't keep awake. You may know perfectly well that it is all imagination, but that sort of thing wears you down if it is kept up night after night."

"You get it regularly every night?"

"Pretty nearly. Its habits are not absolutely regular, however, except that, now you come to mention it, it always gives me Friday night off; if it weren't for that, I should have gone under long ago. When Friday comes I say to it: 'Now, you brute, this is your beastly Sabbath,' and go to bed at eight and sleep the clock round."

"If you care to come down to my nursing home at Hindhead, we can probably keep the creature out of your room and ensure you a decent night's sleep," said Taverner. "But what we really want to know is—," he paused almost imperceptibly, "why your imagination should haunt you with dogs, and not, shall we say, with scarlet snakes in the time-honoured fashion."

"I wish it would," said our patient. "If it was snakes I could 'put more water with it' and drown them, but this slinking black beast—" He shrugged his shoulders and followed the butler out of the room.

"Well, Rhodes, what do you make of it?" asked my colleague after the door closed.

"On the face of it," I said, "it looks like an ordinary example of delusions, but I have seen enough of your queer cases not to limit myself to the internal mechanism of the mind alone. Do you consider it possible that we have another case of thought transference?"

"You are coming along," said Taverner, nodding his head at me approvingly. "When you first enjoined me, you would unhesitatingly have recommended bromide for all the ills the mind is heir to; now you recognize that there are more things in heaven and earth than were taught you in the medical schools.

"So you think we have a case of thought transference? I am inclined to think so too. When a patient tells you his delusions, he stands up for them, and often explains to you that they are psychic phenomena, but when a patient recounts psychic phenomena, he generally apologizes for them, and explains that they are delusions. But why doesn't the creature attack and be done with it, and why does it take its regular half-holiday as if it were under the Shop Hours Act?"

He suddenly slapped his hand down on the desk.

"Friday is the day the Black Lodges meet. We must be on their trail again; they will get to know me before we have finished. Someone who got his occult training in a Black Lodge is responsible for that ghost hound. The reason that Martin gets to sleep in peace on Friday night is that his would-be murderer sits in Lodge that evening and cannot attend to his private affairs."

"His would-be-murderer?" I questioned.

"Precisely. Anyone who sends a haunting like that to a man with a heart like Martin's knows that it means his death sooner or later. Supposing Martin got into a panic and took to his heels when he found the dog behind him in a lonely place?"

95

"He might last for half-a-mile," I said, "but I doubt if he would get any further."

"This is a clear case of mental assassination. Someone who is a trained occultist has created a thought-form of a black hound, and he is sufficiently in touch with Martin to be able to convey it to his mind by means of thought transference, and Martin sees, or thinks he sees, the image that the other man is visualizing.

"The actual thought-form itself is harmless except for the fear it inspires, but should Martin lose his head and resort to vigorous physical means of defence, the effort would precipitate a heart attack, and he would drop dead without the slightest evidence to show who caused his death. One of these days we will raid those Black Lodges, Rhodes; they know too much. Ring up Martin at the Hotel Cecil and tell him we will drive him back with us to-night."

"How do you propose to handle the case?" I asked.

"The house is covered by a psychic bell jar, so the thing cannot get at him while he is under its protection. We will then find out who is the sender, and see if we can deal with him and stop it once and for all. It is no good disintegrating the creature, its master would only manufacture another; it is the man behind the dog that we must get at.

"We shall have to be careful, however, not to let Martin think we suspect he is in any danger, or he will lose his one defence against the creature, a belief in its unreality. That adds to our difficulties, because we daren't question him much, less we rouse his suspicions. We shall have to get at the facts of the case obliquely."

On the drive down to Hindhead, Taverner did a thing I had never heard him do before, talk to a patient about his occult theories. Sometimes, at the conclusion of a case, he would explain the laws underlying the phenomena in order to rid the unknown of its terrors and enable his patient to cope with them, but at the outset, never.

I listened in astonishment, and then I saw what Taverner was fishing for. He wanted to find out whether Martin had any knowledge of occultism himself, and used his own interest to waken the other's—if he had one.

My colleague's diplomacy bore instant fruit. Martin was also interested in these subjects, though his actual knowledge was nil—even I could see that.

"I wish you and Mortimer could meet," he said. "He is an awfully interesting chap. We used to sit up half the night talking of these things at one time."

"I should be delighted to meet your friend," said Taverner. "Do you think he could be persuaded to run down one Sunday and see us? I am always on the lookout for anyone I can learn something from."

"I—I am afraid I could not get hold of him now," said our companion, and lapsed into a preoccupied silence from which all Taverner's conversational efforts failed to rouse him. We had evidently struck some painful subject, and I saw my colleague make a mental note of the fact.

As soon as we got in, Taverner went straight to his study, opened the safe, and took out a card index file.

"Maffeo, Montague, Mortimer," he muttered, as he turned the cards over. "Anthony William Mortimer. Initiated into the Order of the Cowled Brethern, October, 1912; took office as Armed Guard, May, 1915. Arrested on suspicion of espionage, March, 1916. Prosecuted for exerting undue influence in the making of his mother's will. (Everybody seems to go for him, and no one seems to be able to catch him.) Became Grand Master of the Lodge of Set the Destroyer. Knocks, two, three, two, password, 'Jackal.'

"So much for Mr. Mortimer. A good man to steer clear of, I should imagine. Now I wonder what Martin has done to upset him."

As we dared not question Martin, we observed him, and I very soon noticed that he watched the incoming posts with the greatest anxiety. He was always hanging about the hall when they arrived, and seized his scanty mail with eagerness, only to lapse immediately into despondency.

Whatever letter it was that he was looking for never came. He did not express any surprise at this, however, and I concluded that he was rather hoping against hope than expecting something that might happen.

Then one day he could stand it no longer, and as for the twentieth time I unlocked the mailbag and informed him that there was nothing for him, he blurted out: "Do you believe that 'absence makes the heart grow fonder,' Dr. Rhodes?"

"It depends on the nature," I said. "But I have usually observed if you have fallen out with someone, you are more ready to overlook his shortcomings when you have been away from him for a time."

"But if you are fond of someone?" he continued, half-anxiously, half-shamefacedly.

"It is my belief that love cools if it is not fed," I said. "The human mind has great powers of adaptation, and one gets used, sooner or later, to being without one's nearest and dearest."

"I think so, too," said Martin, and I saw him go off to seek consolation from his pipe in a lonely corner.

"So there is a woman in the case," said Taverner when I reported the incident. "I should rather like to have a look at her. I think I shall set up as a rival to Mortimer; if he sends black thought forms, let me see what I can do with a white one."

I guessed that Taverner meant to make use of the method of silent suggestion, of which he was a past-master.

Apparently Taverner's magic was not long in working, for a couple of days later I handed Martin a letter which caused his face to light up with pleasure, and sent him off to his room to read it in private. Half an hour later he came to me in the office and said:

"Dr. Rhodes, would it be convenient if I had a couple of guests to lunch to-morrow?"

I assured him that this would be the case, and noted the

change wrought in his appearance by the arrival of the long wished-for letter. He would have faced a pack of black dogs at that moment.

Next day I caught sight of Martin showing two ladies round the grounds, and when they came into the dining-room he introduced them as Mrs. and Miss Hallam. There seemed to be something wrong with the girl, I thought; she was so curiously distrait and absent-minded. Martin, however, was in the seventh heaven; the man's transparent pleasure was almost amusing to witness. I was watching the little comedy with a covert smile, when suddenly it changed to tragedy.

As the girl stripped her gloves off she revealed a ring upon the third finger of her left hand. It was undoubtedly an engagement ring. I raised my eyes to Martin's face, and saw that his were fixed upon it. In the space of a few seconds the man crumpled; the happy little luncheon party was over. He strove to play his part as host, but the effort was pitiful to watch, and I was thankful when the close of the meal permitted me to withdraw.

I was not allowed to escape however. Taverner caught my arm as I was leaving the room and drew me out on the terrace.

"Come along," he said. "I want to make friends with the Hallam family; they may be able to throw some light on our problem."

We found that Martin had paired off with the mother, so we had no difficulty in strolling round the garden with the girl between us. She seemed to welcome the arrangement, and we had not been together many minutes before the reason was made evident.

"Dr. Taverner," she said, "may I talk to you about myself?"

"I shall be delighted, Miss Hallam," he replied. "What is it you want to ask me about?"

"I am so very puzzled about something. Is it possible to be in love with a person you don't like?"

"Quite possible," said Taverner, "but not likely to be very satisfactory,"

"I am engaged to a man," she said, sliding her engagement ring on and off her finger, "whom I am madly, desperately in love with when he is not there, and as soon as he is present I feel a sense of horror and repulsion for him. When I am away, I long to be with him, and when I am with him, I feel as if everything were wrong and horrible. I cannot make myself clear, but do you grasp what I mean?"

"How did you come to get engaged to him?" asked Taverner.

"In the ordinary way. I have known him nearly as long as I have Billy," indicating Martin, who was just ahead of us, walking with the mother.

"No undue influence was used?" said Taverner.

"No, I don't think so. He just asked me to marry him, and I said I would."

"How long before that had you known that you would accept him if he proposed to you?"

"I don't know. I hadn't thought of it; in fact the engagement was as much a surprise to me as to everyone else. I had never thought of him in that way till about three weeks ago, and then I suddenly realized that he was the man I wanted to marry. It was a sudden impulse, but so strong and clear that I knew it was the thing for me to do."

"And you do not regret it?"

"I did not until to-day, but as I was sitting in the dining room I suddenly felt how thankful I should be if I had not got to go back to Tony."

Taverner looked at me. "The psychic isolation of this house has its uses," he said. Then he turned to the girl again. "You don't suppose that it was Mr. Mortimer's forceful personality that influenced your decision?"

I was secretly amused at Taverner's shot in the dark, and the way the girl walked blissfully into his trap.

"Oh, no," she said, "I often get those impulses; it was on just such a one that I came down here."

"Then," said Taverner, "it may well be on just such another that you got engaged to Mortimer, so I may as well tell you that it was I who was responsible for that impulse."

The girl stared at him in amazement.

"As soon as I knew of your existence I wanted to see you. There is a soul over there that is in my care at present, and I think you play a part in his welfare."

"I know I do," said the girl, gazing at the broad shoulders of the unconscious Martin with so much wistfulness and yearning that she clearly betrayed where her real feelings lay.

"Some people send telegrams when they wish to communicate, but I don't; I send thoughts, because I am certain they will be obeyed. A person may disregard a telegram, but he will act on a thought, because he believes it to be his own; though, of course, it is necessary that he should not suspect he is receiving suggestion, or he would probably turn round and do the exact opposite."

Miss Hallam stared at him in astonishment. "Is such a thing possible?" she exclaimed. "I can hardly believe it."

"You see that vase of scarlet geraniums to the left of the path? I will make your mother turn aside and pick one. Now watch."

We both gazed at the unconscious woman as Taverner concentrated his attention upon her, and sure enough, as they drew abreast of the vase, she turned aside and picked a scarlet blossom.

"What are you doing to our geraniums?" Taverner called to her.

"I am so sorry," she called back, "I am afraid I yielded to a sudden impulse."

"All thoughts are not generated within the mind that thinks them," said Taverner. "We are constantly giving each other unconscious suggestions, and influencing minds without knowing it, and if a man who understands the power of thought deliberately trains his mind in its use, there are few things he cannot do."

We had regained the terrace in the course of our walk, and Taverner took his farewell and retired to the office. I followed him, and found him with the safe open and his card index upon the table.

"Well, Rhodes, what do you make of it all?" he greeted me.

"Martin and Mortimer after the same girl," said I. "And Mortimer uses for his private ends the same methods you use on your patients."

"Precisely," said Taverner. "An excellent object lesson in the ways of black and white occultism. We both study the human mind—we both study the hidden forces of nature; I use my knowledge for healing and Mortimer uses his for destruction."

"Taverner," I said, facing him, "what is to prevent you also from using your great knowledge for personal ends?"

"Several things, my friend," he replied. "In the first place, those who are taught as I am taught are (though I say it who shouldn't) picked men, carefully tested. Secondly, I am a member of an organization which would assuredly exact retribution for the abuse of its training; and, thirdly, knowing what I do, I dare not abuse the powers that have been entrusted to me. There is no such thing as a straight line in the universe; everything works in curves; therefore it is only a matter of time before that which you send out from your mind returns to it. Sooner or later Martin's dog will come home to its master."

Martin was absent from the evening meal, and Taverner immediately enquired his whereabouts.

"He walked over with his friends to the crossroads to put them on the 'bus for Hazlemere," someone volunteered, and Taverner, who did not seem too well satisfied looked at his watch.

"It will be light for a couple of hours yet," he said. "If he is not in by dusk, Rhodes, let me know."

It was a grey evening, threatening storm, and darkness

set in early. Soon after eight I sought Taverner in his study and said: "Martin isn't in yet, doctor."

"Then we had better go and look for him," said my colleague.

We went out by the window to avoid observation on the part of our other patients, and, making our way through the shrubberies, were soon out upon the moor.

"I wish we knew which way he would come," said Taverner. "There is a profusion of paths to choose from. We had better get on to high ground and watch for him with the field-glasses."

We made our way to a bluff topped with wind-torn Scotch firs, and Taverner swept the heather paths with his binoculars. A mile away he picked out a figure moving in our direction, but it was too far off for identification.

"Probably Martin," said my companion, "but we can't be sure yet. We had better stop up here and await events; if we drop down into the hollow we shall lose sight of him. You take the glasses; your eyes are better than mine. How infernally early it is getting dark to-night. We ought to have had another half-hour of daylight."

A cold wind had sprung up, making us shiver in our thin clothes, for we were both in evening dress and hatless. Heavy grey clouds were banking up in the west, and the trees moaned uneasily. The man out on the moor was moving at a good pace, looking neither to right nor left. Except for his solitary figure the great grey waste was empty.

All of a sudden the swinging stride was interrupted; he looked over his shoulder, paused, and then quickened his pace. Then he looked over his shoulder again and broke into a half trot. After a few yards of this he dropped to a walk again, and held steadily on his way, refusing to turn his head.

I handed the glasses to Taverner.

"It's Martin right enough," he said; "and he has seen the dog."

We could make out now the path he was following, and, descending from the hill, set out at a rapid pace to meet him. We had gone about a quarter of a mile when a sound arose in the darkness ahead of us; the piercing, inarticulate shriek of a creature being hunted to death.

Taverner let out such a halloo as I did not think human lungs were capable of. We tore along the path to the crest of a rise, and as we raced down the opposite slope, we made out a figure struggling across the heather. Our white shirt fronts showed up plainly in the gathering dusk, and he headed towards us. It was Martin running for his life from the death hound.

I rapidly outdistanced Taverner, and caught the hunted man in my arms as we literally cannoned into each other in the narrow path. I could feel the played-out heart knocking like a badly-running engine against his side. I laid him flat on the ground, and Taverner coming up with his pocket medicine case, we did what we could.

We were only just in time. A few more yards and the man would have dropped. As I straightened my back and looked round into the darkness, I thanked God that I had not that horrible power of vision which would have enabled me to see what it was that had slunk off over the heather at our approach. That something went I had no doubt, for half a dozen sheep, grazing a few hundred yards away, scattered to give it passage.

We got Martin back to the house and sat up with him. It was touch-and-go with that ill-used heart, and we had to drug the racked nerves into oblivion.

Shortly after midnight Taverner went to the window and looked out.

"Come here, Rhodes," he said. "Do you see anything?"

I declared that I did not.

"It would be a very good thing for you if you did," declared Taverner. "You are much too fond of treating the thought-forms that a sick mind breeds as if, because they have no objective existence, they were innocuous. Now come along and see things from the view-point of the patient."

He commenced to beat a tattoo upon my forehead, using a peculiar syncopated rhythm. In a few moments I became conscious of a feeling as if a suppressed sneeze were working its way from my nose up into my skull. Then I noticed a faint luminosity appear in the darkness without, and I saw that a greyish-white film extended outside the window. Beyond that I saw the Death Hound!

A shadowy form gathered itself out of the darkness, took a run towards the window, and leapt up, only to drive its head against the grey film and fall back. Again it gathered itself together, and again it leapt, only to fall back baffled. A soundless baying seemed to come from the open jaws, and in the eyes gleamed a light that was not of this world. It was not the green luminosity of an animal, but a purplish grey reflected from some cold planet beyond the range of our senses.

"That is what Martin sees nightly," said Taverner, "only in his case the thing is actually in the room. Shall I open a way through the psychic bell jar it is hitting its nose against, and let it in?"

I shook my head and turned away from that nightmare vision. Taverner passed his hand rapidly across my forehead with a peculiar snatching movement.

"You are spared a good deal," he said, "but never forget that the delusions of a lunatic are just as real to him as that hound was to you."

We were working in the office next afternoon when I was summoned to interview a lady who was waiting in the hall. It was Miss Hallam, and I wondered what had brought her back so quickly.

"The butler tells me that Mr. Martin is ill and I cannot see him, but I wonder if Dr. Taverner could spare me a few minutes?"

I took her into the office, where my colleague expressed no surprise at her appearance.

"So you have sent back the ring?" he observed.

"Yes," she said. "How do you know? What magic are you working this time?"

"No magic, my dear Miss Hallam, only common sense. Something has frightened you. People are not often frightened to any great extent in ordinary civilized society, so I conclude that something extraordinary must have happened. I know you to be connected with a dangerous man, so I look in his direction. What are you likely to have done that could have roused his enmity? You have just been down here, away from his influence, and in the company of the man you used to care for; possibly you have undergone a revulsion of feeling. I want to find out, so I express my guess as a statement; you, thinking I know everything, make no attempt at denial, and therefore furnish me with the information I want."

"But, Dr. Taverner," said the bewildered girl, "why do you trouble to do all this when I would have answered your question if you had asked me?"

"Because I want you to see for yourself the way in which it is possible to handle an unsuspecting person," said he. "Now tell me what brought you here."

"When I got back last night, I knew I could not marry Tony Mortimer," she said, "and in the morning I wrote to him and told him so. He came straight round to the house and asked to see me. I refused, for I knew that if I saw him I should be right back in his power again. He then sent up a message to say that he would not leave until he had spoken to me, and I got in a panic. I was afraid he would force his way upstairs, so I slipped out of the back door and took the train down here, for somehow I felt that you understood what was being done to me, and would be able to help. Of course, I know that he cannot put a pistol to my head and force me to marry him, but he has so much influence over me that I am afraid he may make me do it in spite of myself."

"I think," said Taverner, "that we shall have to deal

drastically with Master Anthony Mortimer."

Taverner took her upstairs, and allowed her and Martin to look at each other for exactly one minute without speaking, and then handed her over to the care of the matron.

Towards the end of dinner that evening I was told that a gentleman desired to see the secretary, and went out to the hall to discover who our visitor might be. A tall, dark man with very peculiar eyes greeted me.

"I have called for Miss Hallam," he said.

"Miss Hallam?" I repeated as if mystified.

"Why, yes," he said, somewhat taken aback. "Isn't she here?"

"I will enquire of the matron," I answered.

I slipped back into the dining-room, and whispered to Taverner, "Mortimer is here."

He raised his eyebrows. "I will see him in the office," he said.

Thither we repaired, but before admitting our visitor, Taverner arranged the reading lamp on his desk in such a way that his own features were in deep shadow and practically invisible.

Then Mortimer was shown in. He assumed an authoritative manner. "I have come on behalf of her mother to fetch Miss Hallam home," said he. "I should be glad if you would inform her I am here."

"Miss Hallam will not be returning to-night, and has wired her mother to that effect."

"I did not ask you what Miss Hallam's plans were; I asked you to let her know I was here and wished to see her. I presume you are not going to offer any objection?"

"But I am," said Taverner. "I object strongly."

"Has Miss Hallam refused to see me?"

"I have not inquired."

"Then by what right do you take up this outrageous position?"

"By this right," said Taverner, and made a peculiar sign with his left hand. On the forefinger was a ring of most un-

107

usual workmanship that I had never seen before.

Mortimer jumped as if Taverner had put a pistol to his head; he leant across the desk and tried to distinguish the shadowed features, then his gaze fell upon the ring.

"The Senior of Seven," he gasped, and dropped back a pace. Then he turned and slunk towards the door, flinging over his shoulder such a glance of hate and fear as I had never seen before. I swear he bared his teeth and snarled.

"Brother Mortimer," said Taverner, "the dog returns to its kennel to-night."

"Let us go to one of the upstairs windows and see that he really takes himself off," went on Taverner.

From our vantage point we could see our late visitor making his way along the sandy road that led to Thursley. To my surprise, however, instead of keeping straight on, he turned and looked back.

"Is he going to return?" I said in surprise.

"I don't think so," said Taverner. "Now watch; something is going to happen."

Again Mortimer stopped and looked around, as if in surprise. Then he began to fight. Whatever it was that attacked him evidently leapt up, for he beat it away from his chest; then it circled round him, for he turned slowly so as to face it. Yard by yard he worked his way down the road, and was swallowed up in the gathering dusk.

"The hound is following its master home," said Taverner.

We heard next morning that the body of a strange man had been found near Bramshott. It was thought he had died of heart failure, for there were no marks of violence on his body.

"Six miles!" said Taverner. "He ran well!"

A Daughter of Pan

Taverner looked at a card that had been brought to him. "Rhodes," he said, "if the County take to calling, I shall put up the shutters and write 'Ichabod' upon them, for I shall know that the glory is departed. Now what in the name of Beelzebub, Asmodius, and a few other of my friends to whom you have not been introduced, does this woman want with me?"

Taverner, his methods and his nursing home, were looked upon askance by the local gentry, and as he, for his part, did not care to prescribe for measles and influenza, we seldom came into contact with our neighbours. That my colleague was a man of profound learning and cosmopolitan polish would have availed him nothing at the local tea parties, which judge a man by his capacity to avoid giving offence.

A narrow-hipped, thin lipped woman was ushered into the room. The orderly waves of her golden hair and the perfection of her porcelain complexion bore evidence to the excellence of her maid and the care that was devoted to her toilette. Her clothes had that upholstered effect which is only obtained when the woman is made to fit the garment, not the garment the woman.

"I want to consult you," she said, "about my youngest daughter, she is a great source of anxiety to us. We fear her mind is not developing properly."

"What are her symptoms?" asked Taverner with his most professional manner.

"She was always a difficult child," said the mother. "We had a great deal of trouble with her, so different to the others. Finally we stopped trying to bring her up with them, and got her special governesses and put her under medical supervision."

"Which I suppose included strict discipline," said Taverner.

"Of course," said our visitor. "She has been most carefully looked after; we have left nothing undone, though it has been a great expense, and I must say that the measures we took have been successful up to a point; her terrible outbreaks of wildness and temper have practically ceased, we have seen nothing of them for a year, but her development seems to have been arrested."

"I must see your daughter before I can give an opinion," said Taverner.

"She is out in the car," said her mother. "I will have her brought in."

She appeared in the care of her governess, who looked the excellent disciplinarian she was reported to be. As a Prussian drill sergeant of the old regime, she would have found her *metier*. The girl herself was a most curious study. She was extraordinarily like her mother. There was the same thin figure, though in the case of the mother the angularities had been padded out by art, whereas in the daughter they came glaringly through her garments, which looked as if she had slept in them. Lank, mouse-coloured hair was wound round her head in heavy greasy coils; a muddy complexion, fish-like eyes, and general air of awkwardness and sprawling limbs completed the unpleasing picture.

Huddled up on the sofa between the two women, who seemed to belong to another species, and who discussed her before her face as if she had been an inanimate object, the girl looked a typical low-grade defective. Now, defectives fill me with nothing but disgust, my pity I reserve for their families, but the girl before me did not inspire me with disgust, but only pity. She reminded me of a caged lark in some wretched animal dealer's shop, its feathers dull with dirt and frayed with the bars, apathetic, unhealthy, miserable, which will not sing because it cannot fly. What nature had intended her to be it was impossible to say, for she had been so thoroughly worked over by the two ardent disciplinarians who flanked her that nothing of the original material remained. Her personality displeased them, and they had effectually repressed it, but alas, there was nothing they could put in its place, and they were left with an unensouled automaton which they dragged off to alienist after alienist in the hopeless attempt to get the damage repaired while maintaining the conditions that had done the damage.

I awoke from my abstraction to hear the mother, who evidently had a taste for economy where the ugly duckling was concerned, bargaining shrewdly with Taverner with regard to fees, and he, who was always more interested in the human than the commercial aspect of the work was meeting her more than half way.

"Taverner," I said as soon as the door closed behind them, "what they are paying won't cover her board and keep, let alone treatment. They're not paupers, look at the car. Hang it all, why don't you make 'em fund up?"

"My dear boy," said Taverner mildly, "I have got to undercut the governess or I shouldn't get the job."

"Do you think the job is worth having at that price?" I growled, for I hate to see a man like Taverner imposed upon.

"Hard to say," he replied. "They have driven a square peg into a round hole with such determination that they have split the peg, but to what extent we cannot tell until we have got it out of the hole. But what are your impressions of our new patient? First impressions are generally the truest. What reaction does she awake in you? Those are the best indications in a psychological case."

"She seems to have given life up as a bad job," I replied. "She's an unlovely object, and yet she is not repellent. I don't so much pity her as sympathize with her, there is a difference you know. I can't put it clearer than that."

"You have put it very clearly indeed," said Taverner.

111

"The distinction between pity and sympathy is the touch-stone in this case; we pity that which we ourselves are not, but we sympathize when, but for the grace of God, there goes you or I. You feel kinship for that soul because, whatever the husk of her may have been reduced to, she is 'one of us,' marred in the making."

"And marred with a heavy hand," I added. "I should think it would have been a case of the S.P.C.C., if they had been poor people."

"You are wrong," said Taverner. "It is a case for the S.P.C.A." With which cryptic remark he left me.

The next day the new patient, who answered to the inappropriate name of Diana, appeared. She looked about fifteen, but as a matter of fact was nearer eighteen. Gaunt, slovenly, ungainly, and morose, she had all the furtive ineptitude of a dog that has been ruined by harsh treatment. She was certainly not an addition to the social amenities of the place, and I should not have been surprised if Taverner had segregated her, but he did not seem disposed to, neither did he place her under any supervision, but gave her complete freedom. Unaccustomed to this lack of restraint, she did not seem to know how to employ herself, and slunk about as if at any moment outraged powers might exact retribution for some misdeed.

There was a good deal of comment upon the way our new patient was neglected, and she was certainly not a credit to the establishment, but I began to see what Taverner was driving at. Left entirely to her own devices the girl was beginning to find her level. If she wanted food, she had to prowl into the dining-room somewhere about the time it was being served; when her hands became uncomfortably sticky, she washed them, as the towels bore evidence, for we could not always observe any difference in the hands. And in addition to all this she was thinking and watching all that went on about her.

"She will wake up presently," said Taverner, "and then we shall see how the primitive wild animal will adapt it-

112

self to civilized society."

We were summoned one day by the outraged matron and went along to Diana's den; one could hardly call it a room after she had occupied it for twenty-four hours. As we went down the corridor a strong smell of burning assailed our nostrils, and when we arrived we found the young lady in question sitting cross-legged on the hearth rug wrapped in the bedspread, a bonfire of the whole of her personal belongings smouldering in the fireplace.

"Why have you burnt your clothes?" enquired Taverner, as if this interesting and harmless eccentricity were a daily occurrence.

"I don't like them."

"What is wrong with them?"

"They are not 'me'."

"Come along to the recreation room and dig among the theatrical costumes and see if you can find something you like."

We set off for the recreation room, Diana, swathed in her bedspread, pattering behind Taverner's tall form, and the disgusted matron bringing up the rear of the ridiculous procession. I had no mind to play nursery maid to Miss Diana, so I left them to their own devices and went along the corridor to see a man we had there of the name of Tennant. His was a dreary existence, for, although a charming man when in his normal state, he had made several attempts at suicide, and had been placed with us by his family as a voluntary patient as an alternative to certification and an asylum. He could not be called mad in the ordinary sense of the word, but as one of those curious cases of *tedium vitae*, the desire for life had failed him. What tragedy lay hidden we did not know, for Taverner, unlike the psychoanalysts, never asked questions; he had his own way of finding out what he wanted to know and despised all such clumsy machinery.

To my surprise I found Tennant turning over a pile of music. I elicited by my questioning that he not only had a great love of music, but had studied seriously with a view to making a profession of it. This was news to us, for his family had given no hint of this when they placed him with us, merely leading us to believe that his means were sufficient for existence, but not for any fullness of life, and that he had passively resigned himself to his lot, sinking into a melancholy in consequence.

I told Taverner of this when we were having our usual after-dinner chat in the office, half gossip, half report, which took place nightly while we smoked our cigars. "So," he said, and rose forthwith and went up to Tennant's room, fetched him down, set him at the piano, and bade him play. Tennant, who, started off with a push, went on like an automaton till the impulse died down, played fluently, but without the slightest feeling. I have little sense of music, but this hurdy-gurdy rendering distressed even me. Several of the other patients present in the drawing room made their escape.

At the end of the piece he made no attempt to start another, but sat motionless for a while; Taverner, likewise, sat silent, watching him to see what he would do next, as his custom was with his patients. Tennant slowly twisted round the revolving stool till he sat with his back to the keyboard and his face to us, with his hands hanging limply between his knees, gazing intently at the toes of his shoes. He was a prematurely aged man of thirty-five or thirty-six. His hair iron-grey, his face deeply lined. The brow was low but broad, the mouth full and curving, the eyes set well apart were very bright on the few occasions when the lids were raised sufficiently to let one see them but the ears were the thing that attracted my attention. I had not noticed them before, for when he came to us his hair was rather long, but Matron had fallen upon him with a pair of automatic hair clippers and given him such a shearing that everything now stood revealed, and I saw that the convolutions of the ear were so arranged that they formed a little peak at the apex, that put me in mind of Hawthorne's story

114

of the Marble Fawn and his little tufted ears.

While I was making this inventory Tennant had slowly raised his eyes to ours, and I saw that they were strangely luminous and animal, gleaming green in the shaded lamp, as a dog's will at night.

"I have got a violin in my room," he said in a toneless voice.

It was the first sign of initiative he had shown, and I went off forthwith to fetch his instrument down. Taverner gave him the note on the piano, but he brushed it aside and tuned his fiddle according to his own liking, to some pitch known only to himself. When he first began to play, it sounded horribly flat, but after a few moments we became accustomed to the strange intervals, and, for me at any rate, they began to exercise an extraordinary fascination.

They exercised a fascination for someone else also, for out of a dark corner where she had tucked herself away unobserved by us, Diana came creeping; for a moment I hardly realized who it was, for a profound change had been wrought in her since the morning. Out of the garments available for her in our theatrical wardrobe she had chosen a little green tunic we had had for Puck when we did *A Midsummer Night's Dream*. Someone (I found out afterwards it was Taverner) had 'Bobbed' her hair; long green stockings showed under the tagged edge of the tunic and revealed the lean and angular lines of her limbs. Some freak of imagination carried my mind back to my school days, and as I sat listening to the strange wailing of the violin, in which the voices of sea-gulls and moor-birds and all creatures of barren and windy spaces seemed to be crying and calling to each other, I seemed to see myself coming in from hare and hounds, glowing with the beat of wind and rain, to tub and change in the steam and babel of the dressing-rooms. For a moment, under the magic of that music, the sense of power and prestige was mine again, for I had been a great man in my school, though of the rank and file in my profession. Once again I was Captain of the Games, running my eye over the new boys in the hope of finding something promising, and then in a flash I found the linking idea that had taken my mind back to those dead and gone days—the sprawling limbs in the long green stockings were those of a runner. The lay-on of the muscles, the length of the bones, all denoted speed and spring. She might not be a hopeful sight for a match-making mamma, but she would have rejoiced the heart of a captain of the games.

Matron appeared at the door like an avenging Nemesis; the hour for lights-out was long overpast, but in our absorption in the music we had forgotten it. She looked at me reproachfully; we were usually allies in upholding discipline, but tonight I felt like a rebellious urchin, and wanted to join Tennant and Diana and the other unmanageables in some outrageous escapade against law and order.

The interruption broke the spell. For a moment Diana's eyes flashed, and I thought we were going to be treated to one of the exhibitions of temper we had heard about but not yet seen. They faded, however, to their usual fish-like neutrality, and the gawky female hobbledehoy shambled off at the bidding of authority.

Tennant, however, turned at bay for a minute, recalled from some upland pasture of the spirit where he had found freedom, and much inclined to resent the disturbance. My hand on his arm, and a word of authority in his ear, however, soon restored him to normal, and he too trudged off in the wake of the matron.

"Damn that woman," said Taverner as he secured the windows, "she is no use for this work."

I stepped outside to fasten the shutters, but paused arrested on the threshold.

"By Jove, Taverner," I exclaimed. "Smell this!"

He joined me on the terrace and together we inhaled the odour of a garden in blossom. Frost lay white upon the grass, and the bleak March wind cut keenly, but the air

116

was full of the odour of flowers, with an undercurrent of sun-warmed pine-woods. Something stirred in the shadow of the creepers, and a huge hare shot past us with a scurry of gravel and gained the shelter of the shrubbery.

"Good gracious," I exclaimed. "Whatever brought him here?"

"Ah, what indeed?" said Taverner. "We should know some rather important things if we knew that."

I had hardly reached my room when I was summoned by a loud knocking at the door. I opened it to find one of the patients clad only in his pyjamas.

"There is something wrong in Tennant's room," he said. "I think he is trying to hang himself."

He was right. Tennant, suspended by the cord of his dressing-gown, swung from the cornice pole. We cut him down, and after some hard work at artificial respiration, got him round, and even Taverner was convinced that constant supervision was the only way of dealing with him. Next day he let me send for a male nurse, but the train that brought him also took away the matron, a much-injured woman, not altogether soothed by the generous cheque and excellent testimonial Taverner had bestowed upon her when he dismissed her without either cause or notice.

Such incidents do not cause a three days wonder in a mental home, and we settled down to our routine next morning. Nevertheless I could not get out of my mind the gull-like wailing of the violin and the strange odour of flowers. They seemed to go together, and in some subtle way they had unsettled and disturbed me. Though spring had not shown itself, a spring restlessness was upon me. Unable to endure the closeness of the office, I set wide open the French windows, letting the bitter wind blow over me as I wrestled with the correspondence that had to be got off by the afternoon post.

It was thus Taverner found me, and he surveyed me curiously.

117

"So you heard it too?" he asked.

"Heard what?" I answered impatiently, for my temper was on edge for some unknown reason.

"The call of Pan," said my colleague, as he shut out the whirlwind.

"I am going out," I announced, gathering up the last of the mail. Taverner nodded without comment, for which I was grateful.

What freak possessed me I do not know, but finding Diana curled up on a sofa in the lounge, I called to her as I would to a dog: "Come on, Diana, come for a run," and like a dog she rose and followed me. Forgetting that though a child in mind, she had reached years of woman-hood, forgetting that she had neither coat, hat, nor boots, and for the matter of that, neither had I, I took her with me through the dripping shrubbery to the garden gate.

The sandy road in which the pillar box stood ended in the heather of the moor. Diana advanced tentatively to the edge of the turf and then stood looking back at me. It was so exactly like a dog asking to be taken for a run that I gave myself up to the illusion. "Come on, Diana," I shouted, "Let's have a scamper."

I raced down the path towards her, and with a bound she was off and away over the heather. Away we went as hard as we could go over the soaked black ground into the rolling mists. I was only just able to keep the figure ahead in sight, for she ran like a deer, leaping what I had to plough through.

We went straight across the level plain that had once been the bed of a lake, heading for the Devil's Jumps. Long after I was struggling for my second wind the bounding figure ahead held its pace, and I did not catch up with her until rising ground gave me the advantage. In the little pinewood on its crest she slipped on the twisted roots and came down, rolling over and over like a puppy. I tripped over the waving green legs and came down too, so heavily, however, that I winded myself.

118

We sat up gasping, and looked at each other, and then with one accord burst out laughing. It was the first time I had ever heard Diana laugh. Her eyes were as green as a cat's, and she showed a double row of very sharp white teeth and a pretty pink tongue. It was not human, but it was very fascinating.

We picked ourselves up and trotted home over the heather, and sneaked in at the scullery door while the maids were at tea. I felt rather uncomfortable about the whole business, and sincerely hoped no one had seen my escapade and that Diana would not speak of it.

Speech was not a habit of hers, however, but she was rich in the language of unconscious gesture and speedily announced to the petty world of the nursing home that there was an understanding between us. Her eyes gleamed green on my appearance, and she showed her sharp white teeth and little pink tongue. If she had a tail, she would have wagged it. I found all this rather disconcerting.

Next day, when Taverner and I went down to the post for a breath of fresh air, we found Diana at our heels.

"Your little pet dog, I see," said Taverner, and I mumbled something about transference of libido and fixations.

Taverner laughed. "My dear boy," he said, "she is not sufficiently human to fall in love with you, so don't worry."

At the end of the road Diana repeated her tactics of the previous day.

"What does she want?" demanded Taverner. I felt myself going an uncomfortable scarlet, and Taverner looked at me curiously.

"She wants me to run with her," I said, thinking that the truth was the only possible explanation and that Taverner would understand it.

He did. But his reply was more disconcerting than his question.

"Well, why not?" he said. "Go on, run with her, very good for both of you."

I hesitated, but he would take no denial, and compelled by his will I lumbered off. But Diana saw the difference. Deep had called unto deep the previous day, but now I was one of the Philistines, and she would not run with me. Instead, she trotted in a circle and looked at me with troubled eyes, her pink tongue hidden behind drooping lips. My heart was filled with a furious hatred of Taverner and myself and all created things, and vaulting the fence, I bolted down the shrubbery and took refuge in my own room, from which I did not descend till dinner.

At that meal Diana gazed at me with her odd green eyes that almost seem to say: "Now you know what I have felt like all these years," and I telepathed back, "I do. Damn everybody."

Taverner tactfully refrained from referring to the matter, for which I was devoutly thankful. A week went by and I thought it was forgotten, when suddenly he broke silence.

"I cannot get Diana to run by herself," he said. I squirmed, but wouldn't answer.

He went to the window and drew up the blind. A full moon shone into the room, clashing horribly with the electric light.

"It is the night of the Vernal Equinox," said Taverner, a propos of nothing.

"Rhodes," he said. "I am going to try a very dangerous experiment. If I fail, there will be trouble, and if I succeed there will be a row, so put your coat on and come with me."

In the drawing-room we found Diana, oblivious of the good ladies knitting jumpers round the fire, curled up on a window seat with her nose pressed to the pane. Taverner opened the window, and she slipped out as noiselessly as a cat; we threw our legs over the sill and followed her.

She waited in the shadow of the house as if afraid to advance. The years of discipline had left their mark upon her, and like a caged-bird when the door is left open, she

120

desired freedom, but had forgotten how to fly. Taverner wrapped around her a heavy tweed cape he was carrying, and putting her between us, we set out for the moors. We went by the same route that our wild flight had followed, to the pine wood that rose on its low crest out of the level of the ancient sea bed.

The Scotch firs, with their sparse tufted crests, were too scanty to make a darkness, but threw grotesque goblin shadows on the needle-carpeted ground. In a hollow of the moor a stream made water-noises away out of sight.

Taverner took the cloak from Diana's shoulders and pushed her out into the moonlight. She hesitated, and then fled timidly back to us, but Taverner, glancing at his watch pushed her out again. I was reminded of that wonderful story of jungle life in which the cubs are brought to the Council Rock so that the wolves of the pack may know and recognize them. Diana was being handed over to her own people.

We waited, while the full moon sailed across the heavens in a halo of golden cloud, Taverner glancing at his watch from time to time. The wind had dropped and in the stillness the stream sounded very loud, but though I neither saw nor heard anything, I knew that something was coming towards us through the shadow of the wood. I found myself trembling in every limb, not from fear, but excitement. Something was passing us, something big and massive, and in its train many lesser things of the same nature. Every nerve in my body began to sing, and without my volition, my foot took a step forward. But Taverner's hand on my arm restrained me.

"This is not for you, Rhodes," he said. "You have too much mentality to find your mating here."

Reluctantly I let him check me. The mad fit passed, and as my eyes cleared again I saw the girl in the moonlight, and knew that she too had felt Their coming.

She turned towards Them, half in fear, half in fascination.

They lured her, but she dared not respond. Then I felt that they had surrounded her, and that she could not escape, and then I saw her surrender. She stretched out her hands towards Them, and I was sure that invisible hands clasped hers; then she raised them towards the sky, and the moon seemed to shine straight between the cupped palms into her breast; then she lowered them towards the earth, and dropping on her knee, pressed them to the ground, and sinking lower, pressed her whole body to the earth till her form hollowed the light soil to receive it.

For a while she lay quiet, and then suddenly she sprang up, and flinging out her hands like one diving, was off like an arrow in the wind.

"Quick, after her!" cried Taverner, starting me off with a blow on the shoulder, and like a flash I too was speeding down the heather paths.

But oh, the difference from our last run. Though Diana still ran like a deer, my limbs were of lead. Life seemed without savour, as if there would never again be any zest in it. Only my sense of duty kept my labouring limbs at work, and presently even that proved ineffective. I dropped further and further behind, no second wind came to ease my labouring lungs, and the figure ahead, bounding on feet of the wind, was lost among the heather.

I dropped to the ground gasping, run off my feet in the first burst. As I lay helpless in the heather, my heart pounding in my throat, I seemed to see a great streaming procession like an undisciplined army, passing across the sky. Ragged banners flapped and waved, wild, discordant, but maddening music broke here and there from the motley rout. Furry snouts on human faces, clawed paws on human limbs, green, vine-like hair falling over flashing eyes that gleamed as green, and here and there, half-frightened but half-fascinated human faces, some hanging back though lured along, others giving themselves up to the flight in a wild abandonment of glamour.

I awoke to find Taverner bending over me.

"Thank God," he said, "your eyes are still human."

No Diana appeared next day, and whether Taverner was anxious or not, he would not reveal.

"She will come back to be fed," was all he would vouchsafe.

The following day there was still no sign of her, and I was becoming very uneasy, for the nights were bitter though the days were warm, when, as we sat by the office fire after "lights out," a faint scratching was heard at the window. Taverner immediately rose and opened it, and in slipped Diana, and sank in a heap on the hearth at my feet. But it was not me she turned to, as in my embarrassment I had expected, but the fire. Taverner and I meant nothing to her.

Taverner returned to his chair, and in silence we watched her. Puck's tunic, soaked and tagged and stained out of all recognition, seemed the only possible clothing for the strange, wild, unhuman figure at our feet. Presently she sat up and ran her hands through matted hair, now steaming in the heat, and seeing me through the thatch, showed white teeth and pink tongue in her strange elfin smile, and with a quick bird-like movement, rubbed her head against my knee. After which token of recognition she returned to her enjoyment of the fire.

Taverner rose and quietly left the room. I hardly dared to breathe lest I should break the spell that kept our visitor quiet, and she should do something embarrassing or uncanny; but I need not have troubled. I meant no more to her than the rest of the furniture.

Taverner returned with a laden tray, and Diana's eyes gleamed. She looked much more human eating with a knife and fork. I had expected her to tear her food with her teeth, but ingrained habit remained.

"Diana," said Taverner, after the completion of her meal.

She smiled.

"Aren't you going to say thank you?"

123

She smiled again, and with her quick, birdlike movement, rubbed her head against his knee as she had done against mine, but she did not speak. He stretched out his hand, and began to smooth and stroke the tangled mass of her hair. She snuggled down at his feet, enjoying the caress and the warmth, and presently there arose a low crooning of contentment, very like the purr of a cat.

"We have done it this time!" said Taverner.

After a while, however, Diana seemed to wake up. Her animal needs being satisfied, the human part of her began to reassert itself.

She twisted round, and resting her elbow on Taverner's knee looked up into his face.

"I came back because I was hungry," she said.

Taverner smiled and continued to smooth her hair.

"But I shall go away again," she added with a touch of defiance.

"You shall come and go as you please," said Taverner. "There will be food when you want it and the doors will never be locked."

This seemed to please her, and she became more communicative, evidently wishing to share with us the experience through which she had passed and to receive our wonder and sympathy. That was the human side of her.

"I saw Them," she said.

"We felt Them," said Taverner. "But we did not see Them."

"No," replied Diana. "You would not. But then you see They are my people. I have always belonged to Them but I did not know it, and now They have found me. I shall go back," she repeated again with conviction.

"Were you cold?" asked Taverner.

"No, only hungry," she replied.

Taverner had her belongings removed to a room on the ground floor, whose window, opening on to the shrubbery, permitted her to come and go freely and unobserved. She never slept there, however, but came each night after "lights out" to the office window. We admitted her, fed her, and after basking for a while in the warmth of the hearth, she slipped out again into the night. Weather made no difference to her; out into the wildest gale she went unflinchingly and returned unharmed. Sometimes she would talk to us in her clipped childish sentences, trying to convey to us something of what she saw, but for the most part she kept silence.

At the next full moon, however, she returned bursting with information. *They* had had a wonderful dance, in which she had been allowed to take part. (We knew now why the kitchen-maid, returning from her evening out, had had hysterics all the way up the drive, and wound up with something very like a fit in the servants' hall.) *They* had been so wonderful that she simply had to tell us all about it, and in speaking of Them in her limited vocabulary she used a phrase that another seer of vision had used: They were the Lordly Ones. More she could not tell us; words failed her, and she made strange play with her hands as if moulding a figure in invisible clay. With quick intuition Taverner gave her pencil and paper, and with lightning rapidity there appeared before us the nude figure of a winged being, drawn with amazing vigour and perfect accuracy.

No attempt had ever been made to teach Diana to draw in all the course of her arduous upbringing—it was considered sufficient if she achieved the decencies without aspiring to accomplishments—neither had she had the opportunity of studying anatomy, yet here was a figure rendered with marvellous draftsmanship and the minute accuracy of detail that is only possible in a study from life.

Diana's interest and delight was as great as ours. Here was indeed a discovery, a way of expression for her cramped and stifled soul, and in half an hour the office was strewn with drawings—a whirling snow spirit who seemed to be treading water; a tree-soul, like a gnarled human torso emerging from the trunk of a tree and blending with

125

its branches; fairies, demons, and quaint and engaging animal studies followed each other in bewildering succession. Finally quite worn out with the tension and excitement of it, Diana consented to go to bed for the first time since that strange night of the Vernal Equinox.

Her need of a supply of paper kept Diana at the house, and her need of an audience made her seek human relationships. The artist creates not only for the pleasure of creation, but also for the pleasure of admiration, and Diana, though she might go to the woods, must needs return to her kind to display her spoils.

With her new-found harmony had come the correlation of mind and body; the long limbs no longer sprawled, but had the grace of a deer's. She was as friendly as a puppy where before she had been morose. But alas, her readiness of response exposed her to some painful knocks in the world of warped lives which is a mental home. For a moment she was crushed, and we feared that she might become again that which she had been, but she discovered that a means of retaliation as well as of expression lay in her pencil, and the discovery saved her. She drew portraits of her persecutors, stark naked (for she never drew clothes), with the anatomical detail and accuracy of all her studies, with their usual expression on their faces, but with the expression of their secret souls in every line of their bodies. These portraits appeared in conspicuous places as if by magic, and their effect can be more easily imagined than described.

Diana had found her place in the march of life. She was no longer the outcast, uncouth and unfriendly. Her spontaneous elfin gaiety, which she had brought back from the woods, was a charm in itself; the mouse-coloured hair had taken on a gloss and gleam of gold, the sallow complexion was nut-brown and rose-red, but her springing swaying movement, her amazing vitality, were her chief distinctions.

For she was extraordinarily vital; she drew her life from

the sun and the wind and the earth, and as long as she was allowed to keep in touch with them, she glowed with an inner light, an incandescence of the spirit that blazed but did not consume. She was the most vital thing I have ever seen. The hair of her head was so charged with electricity that it stood out in a light cloud-like aureole. The blood glowed under her skin, and if her hand touched you, sharp magnetic tinglings ran through the bare flesh.

And this strange vitality was not limited to herself, but infected everybody in her immediate neighborhood, and they reacted to it according to temperament; some would go and sit near her as by a fire; others went nearly demented. To me she was lyrical, the wine of life; she went to my head like some intoxicating drug, I got drunk on her and saw the visions of an opium dream; without a word spoken, she lured me from my work, from my duties, from all that was human and civilized, to follow her out on the moor and commune with the beings whose orbit she seemed to have entered upon that fatal night of the Equinox.

I saw that Taverner was worried; he said no word of reproach, but silently picked up the threads I dropped; I also knew that he had cancelled certain engagements and remained at home. I was untrustworthy, and he dared not leave things to me. I loathed myself, but I could no more pull myself together than the drug-taker far gone in morphia.

A form of clairvoyance was growing fast upon me, not the piercing psychic perceptions of Taverner, who saw straight into the inner soul of men and things, but a power to perceive the subtler aspects of matter; I could distinctly see the magnetic field which surrounds every living thing, and could watch the changes in its state; presently I began to be aware of the coming and going of those unseen presences which were the gods that Diana worshipped. A strong wind, hot sun, or the bare uncultivated earth, seemed to bring them very near me, and I felt the great life

127

of the trees. These things fed my soul and strengthened me as the touch of earth always strengthens any child of the Earth-mother.

The days were lengthening towards the longest day; it would soon be three months since Diana returned to her own place, and I began to wonder how much longer Taverner would keep our now entirely cured patient, but he gave no sign. I began to feel, however, that Diana was now no longer a patient, but that I had become one, and that I was being closely watched in anticipation of a crisis that was imminent. Some abscess of the soul had to come to a head before it could be lanced, and Taverner was awaiting the process.

The idea was slowly growing in my mind that I might marry Diana; marriage did not express the relationship I wished to establish, but I could see no other course open to me; I did not wish to possess her, I only wanted our present relationship to continue, and that I should be free to come and go with her without running the gauntlet of censorius eyes. Taverner, I felt, knew this and fought it, and I could not see why. I could understand his objection to my compromising Diana, but I did not see why he should oppose my marriage to her. My brain, however, was in abeyance in these days, my thoughts were a series of pictures fading into each other like a phantasmagoria, and they told me afterwards that my speech had reverted to the simplicities of early childhood.

But still Taverner waited, biding his time.

The crisis came suddenly. As the sun was setting upon the evening of the longest day Diana appeared upon the steps of the office window and beckoned me out. She appeared extraordinarily beautiful, with the burning sky behind her; the bright fluffed hair caught the level light and shone like an aureole as she stood with her strangely eloquent hands beckoning me out into the gathering dusk. I knew that there was in prospect such a race across the heather as had never yet been, and at the end of it I should

128

meet the Powers she worshipped face to face, and that from that meeting my body might return to the house, but my soul would never enter the habitations of men again. It would remain out there in the open, with Diana and her people. I knew all this, and with the inner vision could see the gathering of the clans that was even now taking place.

Diana's hands called to me, and as if drawn by a spell, I rose slowly from my desk. Diana, thing of air, was calling me out to run with her. But I was not a thing of air, I was a man of flesh and blood, and in a flash of revelation I saw Diana as a beautiful woman and I knew that she was not the woman for me; to part of my nature she called, but she did not call to the whole of me, and I knew that the best in me would remain unmated and uncompanioned if I were to join Diana.

It did Diana no harm to return to Nature, because she was not capable of greater things, but there was more in me than the instincts, and I might not so return without loss to my higher self. The room was lined with books, the door leading into the laboratory stood open and the characteristic smell of the blended drugs came to me. "Smells are surer than sights or sounds to make your heartstrings crack." Had the wind been the other way, had the smell of the pines blown in at the open window, I think I should have gone with Diana, but it was the odour of the laboratory that came to me, and with it the memory of all that I had hoped to make of my life, and I dropped back into my chair and buried my face in my arms.

When I raised my head again the last light of the sunset had gone, and so had Diana.

That night my sleep was heavy and dreamless, which was a great relief, for of late it had been troubled by strange, almost physical impressions, the phantasies of the day becoming the realities of the darkness; but with my rejection of Diana a spell seemed to break, and when I awoke in the morning it was to a normality to which I had been a stranger for many a day. My grip on the organization of

129

the home had come back to me, and I felt as one who had been in exile in a foreign country and has at length returned to his native land.

Diana I did not see for several days for she had again taken to the heather, and rumours of raids upon gardens and fowl houses by a particularly ingenious and elusive gypsy explained why she did not even return to be fed.

My conscience pricking me for my recent lapse, I took upon myself the somewhat arduous task of taking Tennant out for walks, for since his attempt at suicide we had not dared to let him go about alone. It was a dreary business, for Tennant never spoke unless he was addressed, and then only employed the unavoidable minimum of speech. He had certainly made no progress during the months he had been at the nursing home, and I was surprised that Taverner had kept him so long, for he usually declined to keep any case which he considered hopeless. I therefore concluded that he had hopes for Tennant, though in what direction they lay he did not confide to me.

We swung over the heather paths in the direction of Frensham, and I suddenly realized to my annoyance, that we were following Diana's favourite trail to the little fir-wood of magic and ill omen. I would willingly have avoided it if I could, for I did not wish to be reminded of certain incidents which I felt it was better for my peace of mind that I should forget, but there was no alternative unless we waded for a mile or two through knee-deep heather. In the light shadow of the trees we paused, Tennant gazing up the long shafts of the trunks into the dark tufted crests that looked like islands in the sky.

"Wendy's house in the tree tops!" I heard him say to himself, oblivious of my presence, and I guessed that his weary soul would love to sleep for ever in the rocking cradle of the branches. The sun drew all the incense from the firs, and the sky had that intense Italian blue that is often seen over these great wastes; a warm wind blew softly over the heather, bringing the sound of innumerable bees and far-away sheep; we flung ourselves down on the sun-warmed earth, and even Tennant, for once, seemed happy. As for me, every breath I drew of that warm radiant air brought peace and healing to my spirit.

Tennant, propped against a tree, hat off, shirt open, and head thrown back against the rough red bark, sat gazing into the blue distance and whistling softly between his teeth. I lay flat on my back among the pine needles, and I think I went to sleep. At any rate I never heard the approach of Diana, nor was aware of her presence until I raised my head. She lay at Tennant's feet gazing into his face with the unblinking steadiness of an animal, and he was whistling as softly as before, but with an exquisite, flute-like tone, those strange cadences of his that had been the origin of all my trouble. I thought of the older Greek world of centaurs and Titans, who ranged and ruled before Zeus and his court made heaven human. Tennant was not even primitive, he was pre-Adamic. As for Diana, she was no daughter of Eve, but of the Dark Lilith who preceded her, and I realized that those two were of the same world and belonged to each other. A twinge of the old wound shot through me at this realization, and also a twinge of envy, for theirs was a happier lot than our civilized bondage, but I lay quiet, watching their idyll.

The shadows of the firs lay far out over the heather before I roused Tennant for our return to earth, and as we came back through the golden evening light, Diana came with us.

When I told Taverner of this incident, over our usual after-dinner smoking, half report, half gossip, I saw that it was no surprise to him.

"I hoped that would happen," he said. "It is the only possible solution to the case that I can think of, but what will her family say?"

"I think they will say, 'Praise the Lord,' and economise over her trousseau," I replied, and my prophecy proved correct.

It was the queerest wedding I ever saw. The parson, thoroughly uncomfortable, but afraid to refuse to perform the ceremony; the upholstered mother and her friends trying hard to do the thing properly; the bridegroom's relatives, whose attempt to get him certified at the eleventh hour had been baulked by Taverner, furiously watching ten thousand pounds of trust moneys passing out of their keeping; a bride who looked like a newly-caught wild thing, and who would have bolted out of the church if Taverner had not shown her very clearly that he was prepared for such a manoeuvre and would not permit it; and a bridegroom who was far away in some heaven of his own, and upon whose face was a glory that never shone on land or sea.

The departure of the happy couple upon their honeymoon was a sight for the gods, whom I am convinced were present. All the wedding guests in their wedding garments were drawn up about the front door, when out came Diana in her Puck's tunic and bolted like a rabbit down the drive; at a more sober pace followed her spouse leading a donkey upon who back was packed a tent and from whose flanks dangled cooking pots.

Surrounded by the broadcloth of the men and the silks of the women, and against the background of the clipped laurels of the shrubbery they looked incongruous, daft, degenerate, everything their relatives said they were, but the minute they had passed the gate and set foot upon the black soil of the moor, there was a change. Great Presences came to meet them, and whether they perceived Them or not, a silence fell upon the wedding party.

In ten seconds the moor took them, man, girl, and donkey fading into its grey-browns in the most amazing fashion, as if they had simply ceased to exist. They had gone to their own place, and their own place had made them welcome. A civilization with which they had nothing to do would never again have the power to torture and imprison them for being different. In dead silence the

132

wedding party went in to eat its wedding breakfast and no one remembered to give any toasts.

We heard no more of the wayfarers until the following spring, when there came a tap upon the office window after "lights out," which instantly put me in mind of Diana. It was not she, however, but her husband. Taverner was absent, but in response to a brief request I accompanied my summoner. We had not far to go; the little brown tent was pitched almost under the lea of our wood, and I saw in an instant why I had been summoned, though there was little need to summon me, for the Nature-gods can look after their own, it is only we superior beings who have to be dragged into the world by the scruff of our necks; the gates of life swung upon easy hinges, and in a few minutes a little granddaughter of Pan lay in my hands, a little, new-made perfection, save for the tufted ears. I wondered what new breed of mortals had been introduced into our troubled old world to disturb its civilization.

"Oh, Taverner," I thought, "what will the future hold you responsible for? Will it rank you with the man who introduced rabbits into Australia...or with Prometheus?"

The Subletting of the Mansion

"Build thou more stately mansions, O my soul—"

The post bag of the nursing home was always sent to the village when the gardeners departed at six, so if any belated letter-writer desired to communicate with the outer world at a later hour, he had to walk to the pillar box at the cross roads with his own missives. As I had little time for my private letter-writing during the day, the dusk usually saw me with a cigar and a handful of letters taking my after-dinner stroll in that direction.

It was not my custom to encourage the patients to accompany me on these strolls, for I felt that I did my duty towards them during working hours, and so was entitled to my leisure, but Winnington was not quite in the position of an ordinary patient, for he was a personal friend of Taverner's, and also, I gathered, a member of one of the lesser degrees of that great fraternity of whose work I had had some curious glimpses; and so the fascination which this fraternity always had for me, although I have never aspired to its membership, together with the amusing and bizarre personality of the man, made me meet half way his attempt to turn our professional relationship into a personal one.

Therefore it was that he fell into step with me down the long path that ran through the shrubbery to the little gate, at the far end of the nursing home garden, which gave upon the cross roads where the pillar box stood.

Having posted our letters, we were lounging back across the road when the sound of a motor horn made us start

134

aside, for a car swung round the corner almost on top of us. Within it I caught a glimpse of a man and woman, and on top was a considerable quantity of luggage.

The car turned in at the gate of a large house whose front drive ran out at the cross roads, and I remarked to my companion that I supposed Mr. Hirschmann, the owner of the house, had got over his internment and come back to live there again, for the house had stood empty, though furnished, since a trustful country had decided that its confidence might be abused, and that the wily Teuton would bear watching.

Meeting Taverner on the terrace as we returned to the house, I told him that Hirschmann was back again, but he shook his head.

"That was not the Hirschmanns you saw," he said, "but the people they have let the house to. Bellamy, I think their name is, they have taken the place furnished; either one or other of them is an invalid, I believe."

A week later I was again strolling down to the pillar box when Taverner joined me, and smoking vigorously to discourage the midges, we wandered down to the cross roads together. As we reached the pillar box a faint creak attracted our attention, and looking round, we saw that the large iron gates barring the entrance to Hirschmann's drive had been pushed ajar and a woman was slipping softly through the narrow opening they afforded. She was obviously coming to the post, but seeing us, hesitated; we stood back, making way for her, and she slipped across the intervening gravel on tip-toe, posted her letter, half bowed to us in acknowledgement of our courtesy, and vanished silently as she had come.

"There is a tragedy being worked out in that house," remarked Taverner.

I was all interest, as I always am, at any manifestation of my chief's psychic powers, but he merely laughed.

"Not clairvoyance this time, Rhodes, but merely common sense. If a woman's face is younger than her figure,

135

then she is happily married; if the reverse, then she is working out a tragedy."

"I did not see her face," I said, "but her figure was that of a young woman."

"I saw her face," said Taverner, "and it was that of an old one."

His strictures upon her were not entirely justified, however, for a few nights later Winnington and I saw her go to the post again, and although her face was heavily lined and colourless, it was a very striking one, and the mass of auburn hair that surrounded it seemed all the richer for its pallor. I am afraid I stared at her somewhat hard, trying to see the signs from which Taverner had deduced her history. She slipped out through the scarcely opened gate, moving swiftly but stealthily, as one accustomed to need concealment, gave us a sidelong glance under long dark lashes, and retreated as she had come.

It was the complete immobility of the man at my side which drew my attention to him. He stood rooted to the ground, staring up the shadowed drive where she had disappeared as if he would send his very soul to illuminate the darkness. I touched his arm. He turned to speak, but caught his breath, and the words were lost in the bubbling cough that means haemorrhage. He threw one arm round my shoulders to support himself, for he was a taller man than I, and I held him while he coughed up the scarlet arterial blood which told its own story.

I got him back to the house and put him to bed, for he was very shaky after his attack, and reported what had happened to Taverner.

"I don't think he is going to last long," I said.

My colleague looked surprised. "There is a lot of life in him," he said.

"There is not much left of his lungs," I answered, "and you cannot run a car without an engine."

Winnington was not laid up long, however, and the first day we let him out of bed he proposed to go to the post

136

with me. I demurred, for it was some little distance there and back, but he took me by the arm and said: "Look here, Rhodes, I've *got* to go."

I asked the reason for so much urgency. He hesitated, and then he burst out, "I want to see that woman again."

"That's Mrs. Bellamy," I said. "You had better let her alone; she is not good for you. There are plenty of nice girls on the premises you can flirt with if you want to. Let the married women alone; the husbands only come round and kick up a row, and it is bad for the nursing home's reputation."

But Winnington was not to be headed off.

"I don't care whose wife she is; she's the woman I—I— never thought I should see," he finished lamely. "Hang it all, man, I am not going to speak to her or make an ass of myself, I only want to have a look at her. Any way, I don't count, I have pretty nearly finished with this sinful flesh, what's left of it."

He swayed before me in the dusk; tall, gaunt as a skeleton, with a colour in his cheeks we should have rejoiced to see in any other patient's, but which was a danger signal in his.

I knew he would go, whether I consented or not, so I judged it best we should go together; and thereafter it became an established thing that we should walk to the cross roads at post time whether there were letters or not. Sometimes we saw Mrs. Bellamy slip silently out to the post, and sometimes we did not. If we missed her for more than two days, Winnington was in a fever, and when for five consecutive days she did not appear, he excited himself into another haemorrhage and we put him to bed, too weak to protest.

It was while telling Taverner of this latest development that the telephone bell rang. I, being nearest the instrument, picked it up and took the message.

"Is that Dr. Taverner?" said a woman's voice.

"This is Dr. Taverner's nursing home," I replied.

137

"It is Mrs. Bellamy of Headington House who is speaking. I should be grateful if Dr. Taverner would come and see my husband; he has been taken suddenly ill."

I turned to give the message to Taverner, but he had left the room. A sudden impulse seized me.

"Dr. Taverner is not here at the moment," I said; "but I will come over if you like. I am his assistant; my name is Rhodes, Dr. Rhodes."

"I should be very grateful," replied the voice. "Can you come soon? I am anxious!"

I picked up my cap and went down the path I had so often followed with Winnington. Poor chap, he would not stroll with me again for some time, if ever. At the cross roads I paused for a moment, marvelling that the invisible barrier of convention was at last lowered and that I was free to go up the drive and speak with the woman I had so often watched in Winnington's company. I pushed the heavy gates ajar just as she had done, walked up the deeply shaded avenue, and rang the bell.

I was shown into a sort of morning room where Mrs. Bellamy came to me almost immediately.

"I want to explain matters to you before you see my husband," she said. "The housekeeper is helping me with him, and I do not want her to know; you see the trouble—I am afraid—is drugs."

So Taverner had been right as usual, she was working out a tragedy.

"He has been in a stupor all day, and I am afraid he has taken an overdose; he has done so before, and I know the symptoms. I felt that I could not get through the night without sending for someone."

She took me to see the patient and I examined him. His pulse was feeble, breathing difficult, and colour bad, but a man who is as inured to the drug as he seemed to be is very hard to kill, more's the pity. I told her what measures to take; said I did not anticipate any danger, but she could phone me again if a change took place.

As she wished me good-bye she smiled, and said: "I know you quite well by sight, Dr. Rhodes; I have often seen you at the pillar box."

"It is my usual evening walk," I replied. "I always take the letters that have missed the post bag."

I was in two minds about telling Winnington of my interview, wondering whether the excitement into which it would throw him or his continued suspense would be the lesser of the two evils, and finally decided in favour of the former. I went up to his room when I got back, and plunged into the matter without preamble.

"Winnington," I said, "I have seen your divinity."

He was all agog in a minute, and I told him of my interview, suppressing only the nature of the illness, which I was in honour bound not to reveal. This, however, was the point he particularly wished to know, although he knew that I naturally could not tell him. Finding me obdurate, he suddenly raised himself in bed, seized my hand, and laid it to his forehead.

"No, you don't!" I cried, snatching it away, for I had by now seen enough of Taverner's methods to know how thought-reading was done, but I had not been quick enough, and Winnington sank back on the pillowless bed chuckling.

"Drugs!" he said, and breathless from his effort, could say no more; but the triumph in his eyes told me that he had learnt something which he considered of vital importance.

I went round next morning to see Bellamy again. He was conscious, regarded me with sulky suspicion, and would have none of me, and I saw that my acquaintance with his household was likely to end as it had begun, at the pillar box.

An evening or two later Mrs. Bellamy and I met again at the cross roads. She answered my greeting with a smile, evidently well enough pleased to have some one to speak to beside her boorish husband, for they seemed to know no one in the district.

She commented on my solitary state. "What has become of the tall man who used to come with you to the post?" she enquired.

I told her of poor Winnington's condition.

Then she said a curious thing for one who was a comparative stranger to me, and a complete stranger to Winnington.

"Is he likely to die?" she asked, looking me straight in the face with a peculiar expression in her eyes.

Surprised by her question, I blurted out the truth.

"I thought so," she said. "I am Scotch, and we have second sight in our family, and last night I saw his wraith."

"You saw his wraith?" I exclaimed mystified.

She nodded her auburn head. "Just as clearly as I see you," she replied. "In fact he was so distinct that I thought he must have been another doctor from the nursing home whom you had sent over in your stead to see how my husband was getting on.

"I was sitting beside the bed with the lamp turned low, when a movement caught my notice, and I looked up to see your friend standing between me and the light. I was about to speak to him when I noticed the extraordinary expression of his face, so extraordinary that I stared at him and could find no word to say, for he seemed to be absolutely gloating over me—or my husband—I could not tell which.

"He was standing up straight, not his usual stoop." ('So you have been watching him too!' I thought.) "And his face wore a look of absolute triumph, as if he had at last won something for which he had waited and worked for a very long time, and he said to me quite slowly and distinctly: 'It will be my turn next.' I was just about to answer him and ask what he meant by his extraordinary behaviour, when I suddenly found that I could see the lamp *through* him, and before I had recovered from my surprise he had vanished. I took it to mean that my husband would

140

live, but that he himself was dying."

I told her that from my knowledge of the two cases her interpretation was likely to prove a true one, and we stood for some minutes telling ghosts stories before she returned through the iron gates.

Winnington was slowly pulling round from his attack, though as yet unable to leave his bed. His attitude concerning Mrs. Bellamy had undergone a curious change; he still asked me each day if I had seen her at the pillar box and what she had had to say for herself, but he showed no regret that he was not well enough to accompany me thither and make her acquaintance; instead, his attitude seemed to convey that he and she were partners in some secret in which I had no share.

Although he was over the worst, his last attack had so pulled him down that his disease had got the upper hand, and I saw that it was unlikely that he would ever get out of bed again, so I indulged his foible in regard to Mrs. Bellamy, feeling sure that no harm could come of it. Her visits to the pillar box, what she said, and what I said were duly reported for the benefit of the sick man, whose eyes twinkled with a secret amusement while I talked. As far as I could make out, for he did not give me his confidence, he was biding his time till Bellamy took another overdose, and I should have felt considerable anxiety as to what he intended to do then had I not known that he was physically incapable of crossing the room without assistance. Little harm could come, therefore, from letting him daydream, so I did not seek to fling cold water on his fantasies.

One night I was aroused by a tap at my door and found the night nurse standing there. She asked me to come with her to Winnington's room, for she had found him unconscious, and his condition gave her anxiety. I went with her, and as she had said, he was in a state of coma, pulse imperceptible, breathing almost nonexistent; for a moment I was puzzled at the turn his illness had taken, but as I stood looking down at him, I heard the faint click in the

141

throat followed by the long sibilant sigh that I had so often heard when Taverner was leaving his body for one of those strange psychic expeditions of his, and I guessed that Winnington was at the same game, for I knew that he had belonged to Taverner's fraternity and had doubtless learnt many of its arts.

I sent the nurse away and settled myself to wait beside our patient as I had often waited beside Taverner; not a little anxious, for my colleague was away on his holiday, and I had the responsibility of the nursing home on my shoulders; not that that would have troubled me in the ordinary way, but occult matters are beyond my ken, and I knew that Taverner always considered that these psychic expeditions were not altogether unaccompanied by risk.

I had not a long vigil, however; after about twenty minutes I saw the trance condition pass into natural sleep, and having made sure that the heart had taken up its beat again and that all was well, I left my patient without rousing him and went back to bed.

Next morning, as Winnington did not refer to the incident, I did not either, but his ill-concealed elation showed that something had transpired upon that midnight journey which had pleased him mightily.

That evening when I went to the pillar box I found Mrs. Bellamy there waiting for me. She began without preamble:

"Dr. Rhodes, did your tall friend die during the night?"

"No," I said, looking at her sharply. "In fact he is much better this morning."

"I am glad of that," she said, "for I saw his wraith again last night, and wondered if anything had happened to him."

"What time did you see him?" I enquired, a sudden suspicion coming into my mind.

"I don't know," she replied; "I did not look at the clock, but it was some time after midnight; I was wakened by something touching my cheek very softly, and thought the

142

cat must have got into the room and jumped on the bed; I roused myself, intending to put it out of the room, when I saw something shadowy between me and the window; it moved to the foot of the bed, and I felt a slight weight on my feet, more than that of a cat, about what one would expect from a good-sized terrier, and then I distinctly saw your friend sitting on the foot of the bed, watching me. As I looked at him, he faded and disappeared, and I could not be sure that I had not imagined him out of the folds of the eiderdown, which was thrown back over the footboard, so I thought I would ask you whether there was—anything to account for what I saw."

"Winnington is not dead," I said. And not wishing to be questioned any further in the matter, wished her good night somewhat abruptly and was turning away when she called me back.

"Dr. Rhodes," she said, "my husband has been in that heavy stupor all day; do you think that anything ought to be done?"

"I will come and have a look at him if you like," I answered. She thanked me, but said she did not want to call me in unless it were essential, for her husband so bitterly resented any interference.

"Have you got a butler or valet in the house, or is your husband alone with you and the women servants?" I enquired, for it seemed to me that a man who took drugs to the extent that Bellamy did was not the safest, let alone the pleasantest company for three or four women.

Mrs. Bellamy divined my thought and smiled sadly. "I am used to it," she said. "I have always coped with him single-handed."

"How long has he been taking drugs?" I asked.

"Ever since our marriage," she replied. "But how long before that I cannot tell you."

I did not like to press her any further, for her face told me of the tragedy of that existence, so I contented myself with saying:

143

"I hope you will let me know if you need help at any time. Dr. Taverner and I do not practise in this district, but we would gladly do what we could in an emergency."

As I went down the shrubbery path I thought over what she had told me. Taking into consideration that Winnington had been in a trance condition between two and two-thirty, I felt certain that what she had seen was no phantasy of her imagination. I was much puzzled how to act. It seemed to me that Winnington was playing a dangerous game, dangerous to himself, and to the unsuspecting woman on whom he was practising, yet if I spoke to him on the matter, he would either laugh at me or tell me to mind my own business, and if I warned her, she would regard me as a lunatic. By refusing to admit their existence, the world gives a very long start to those who practice the occult arts.

I decided to leave matters alone until Taverner came back, and therefore avoided deep waters when I paid my evening visits to Winnington. As usual he enquired for news of Mrs. Bellamy, and I told him that I had seen her, and casually mentioned that her husband was bad again. In an instant I saw that I had made a mistake and given Winnington information that he ought not to have had, but I could not unsay my words, and took my leave of him with an uneasy feeling that he was up to something that I could not fathom. Very greatly did I wish for Taverner's experience to take the responsibility off my shoulders, but he was away in Scotland, and I had no reasonable grounds for disturbing his well-earned holiday.

About an hour later, as I had finished my rounds and was thinking of bed, the telephone bell rang. I answered, and heard Mrs. Bellamy's voice at the end of the line.

"I wish you would come round, Dr. Rhodes," she said, "I am very uneasy."

In a few minutes I was with her, and we stood together looking at the unconscious man on the bed. He was a powerfully built fellow of some thirty-five years of age, and before the drug had undermined him, must have been a fine-looking man. His condition appeared to be the same as before, and I asked Mrs. Bellamy what it was that had rendered her so anxious, for I had gathered from the tone of her voice over the phone that she was frightened.

She beat about the bush for a minute or two, and then the truth came out.

"I am afraid my nerve is going," she said. "But there seems to be something or somebody in the room, and it was more than I could stand alone; I simply had to send for you. Will you forgive me for being so foolish and troubling you at this hour of the night?"

I quite understood her feelings, for the strain of coping with a drug maniac in that lonely place with no friends to help her—a strain which I gathered, had gone on for years—was enough to wear down anyone's courage.

"Don't think about that," I said. "I'm only too glad to be able to give you any help I can; I quite understand your difficulties."

So, although her husband's condition gave no cause for anxiety, I settled down to watch with her for a little while, and do what I could to ease the strain of the intolerable burden.

We had not been sitting quietly in the dim light for very long before I was aware of a curious feeling. Just as she had said, we were not alone in the room. She saw my glance questing into the corners, and smiled.

"You feel it too?" she said. "Do you see anything?"

"No," I answered, "I am not psychic, I wish I were; but I tell you who will see it, if there is anything to be seen, and that is my dog; he followed me here, and is curled up in the porch if he has not gone home. With your permission I will fetch him up and see what he makes of it."

I ran down stairs and found the big Airedale, whose task it was to guard the nursing home, patiently waiting on the mat. Taking him into the bedroom, I introduced him to Mrs. Bellamy, whom he received with favour, and then,

145

leaving him to his own devices, sat quietly watching what he would do. First he went over to the bed and sniffed at the unconscious man, then he wandered round the room as a dog will in a strange place, and finally he settled down at our feet in front of the fire. Whatever it was that had disturbed our equanimity he regarded as unworthy of notice.

He slept peacefully till Mrs. Bellamy, who had brewed tea, produced a box of biscuits, and then he woke up and demanded his share; first he come to me, and received a contribution, and then he walked quietly up to an empty arm chair and stood gazing at it in anxious expectancy. We stared at him in amazement. The dog, serenely confident of his reception, pawed the chair to attract its attention. Mrs. Bellamy and I looked at each other.

"I had always heard," she said, "that it was only cats who liked ghosts, and that dogs were afraid of them."

"So had I," I answered. "But Jack seems to be on friendly terms with this one."

And then the explanation flashed into my mind. If the invisible presence were Winnington, whom Mrs. Bellamy had already seen twice in that very room, then the dog's behaviour was accounted for, for Winnington and he were close friends, and the presence which to us was so uncanny, would, to him, be friendly and familiar.

I rose to my feet. "If you don't mind," I said, "I will just go round to the nursing home and attend to one or two things, and then we will see this affair through together."

I raced back through the shrubberies to the nursing home, mounted the stairs three at a time, and burst into Winnington's bedroom. As I expected, he was in deep trance.

"Oh you devil!" I said to the unconscious form on the bed, "what games are you up to now? I wish to Heaven that Taverner were back to deal with you."

I hastened back to Mrs. Bellamy, and to my surprise, as I re-entered her room I heard voices, and there was Bellamy, fully conscious, and sitting up in bed and drinking

146

tea. He looked dazed, and was shivering with cold, but had apparently thrown off all effects of his drug. I was nonplussed, for I had counted on slipping away before he had recovered consciousness, for I had in mind his last reception of me which had been anything but cordial, but it was impossible to draw back.

"I am glad to see you are better, Mr. Bellamy," I said. "We have been rather anxious about you."

"Don't you worry about me, Rhodes," was the reply. "Go back to bed, old chap; I'll be as right as a trivet as soon as I get warm."

I withdrew; there was no further excuse for my presence, and back I went to the nursing home again to have another look at Winnington. He was still in a state of coma, so I settled down to watch beside him, but hour after hour went by while I dozed in my chair, and finally the grey light of dawn came and found his condition still unchanged. I had never known Taverner to be out of his body for such a length of time, and Winnington's condition worried me considerably. He might be all right; on the other hand, he might not; I did not know enough about these trances to be sure, and I could not fetch Taverner back from his holiday on a wild goose chase.

The day wore itself away, and when night found Winnington still in the same state I decided that the time had come for some action to be taken, and went to the dispensary to get the strychnine, intending to give him an injection of that and see if it would do any good.

The minute I opened the dispensary door I knew there was someone there, but when I switched on the light the room stood empty before me. All the same, a presence positively jostled my elbow as I searched among the shelves for what I required, and I felt its breath on my neck as I bent over the instrument drawer for the hypodermic syringe.

"Oh Lord!" I said aloud. "I wish Taverner would come back and look after his own spooks. Here, you, whoever

147

you are, go on, clear out, go home; we don't want you here!" And hastily gathering up my impedimenta, I beat a retreat and left it in possession of the dispensary.

My evil genius prompted me to look over my shoulder as I went down the passage, and there, behind me, was a spindle-shaped drift of grey mist some seven feet high. I am ashamed to admit it, but I ran. I am not easily scared by anything I can see, but these half-seen things that drift to us out of another existence, whose presence one can detect but not locate, fill me with cold horror.

I slammed and locked Winnington's door behind me and paused to recover my breath; but even as I did so, I saw a pool of mist gathering on the floor, and there was the creature, oozing through the crack under the door and re-forming itself in the shadow of the wardrobe.

What would I not have given for Taverner's presence as I stood there, helplessly watching it, syringe in hand, sweating like a frightened horse. Then illumination suddenly burst upon me; what a fool I was, of course it was Winnington coming back to his body!

"Oh Lord!" I said. "What a fright you gave me! For goodness sake get back into your body and stop there, and we'll let bygones be bygones."

But it did not heed my adjuration; it seemed as if it were the hypodermic syringe that attracted it, and instead of returning to its physical vehicle, it hung round me.

"Oh," I said. "So it is the strychnine you are after? Well then, get back into your body and you shall have some. Look, I am going to give your body an injection. Get back inside it if you want any strychnine."

The grey wraith hung for a moment over the unconscious form on the bed, and then, to my unspeakable relief, slowly merged into it, and I felt the heart take up its beat and breathing recommence.

I went to my room dead beat, for I had had no sleep and much anxiety during the past forty-eight hours, so I left a note on my mat to say that I was not to be disturbed in the morning; I felt I had fairly earned my rest, I had pulled two tricky cases through, and put my small knowledge of occultism to a satisfactory test.

But in spite of my instructions I was not left undisturbed. At seven o'clock the matron routed me out.

"I wish you would come and look at Mr. Winnington, Doctor; I think he has gone out of his mind."

I wearily put on my clothes and dipped my heavy head in the basin and went to inspect Winnington. Instead of his usual cheery smile, he greeted me a malign scowl.

"I should be very glad," he said, "if you would kindly tell me where I am."

"You are in your own room, old chap," I said. "You have had a bad turn, but are all right again now."

"Indeed," he said. "This is the first I have heard of it. And who may you be?"

"I'm Rhodes," I replied. "Don't you know me?"

"I know you right enough. You are Dr. Taverner's understrapper at that nursing home place. I suppose my kind friends have put me here to get me out of the way. Well, I can tell you this, they can't make me stop here. Where are my clothes? I want to get up."

"Your clothes are wherever you put them," I replied. "We have not taken them away; but as for getting up, you are not fit to do so. We have no wish to keep you here against your will, and if you want to be moved we will arrange it for you, but you will have to have an ambulance, you have been pretty bad you know." It was my intention to play for time till this sick mood should have passed, but he saw through my manoeuvre.

"Ambulance be damned," he said. "I will go on my own feet." And forthwith he sat up in bed and swung his legs over the edge. But even this effort was too much for him, and he would have slid to the floor if I had not caught him. I called the nurse, and we put him to bed, incapable of giving any further trouble for the moment.

I was rather surprised at this ebullition as coming from

149

Winnington, who had always shown himself a very sweet-tempered, gentle personality, though liable to fits of depression, which, however, were hardly to be wondered at in his condition. He had not much to make him cheerful, poor chap, and but for Taverner's intervention he would probably have ended his days in an infirmary.

When I went down to the pillar box that evening, there was Mrs. Bellamy, and to my surprise, her husband was with her. She greeted me with constraint, watching her husband to see how he would take it, but his greeting lacked nothing in the way of cordiality; one would have thought that I was an old friend of the family. He thanked me for my care of him, and for my kindness to his wife, whom, he said, he was afraid had been going through rather a bad time lately.

"I am going to take her away for a change, however, a second honeymoon, you know; but when we get back I want to see something of you, and also of Dr. Taverner. I am very anxious to keep in touch with Taverner."

I thanked him, marvelling at his change of mood, and only hoping for his wife's sake that it would last; but drug takers are broken reeds to lean upon and I feared that she would have to drain her cup to the dregs.

When I got back to the nursing home I was amazed to find Taverner there.

"Why, what in the world has brought you back from your holiday?" I demanded.

"You did," he replied. "You kept on telepathing S.O.S. messages, so I thought I had better come and see what was the matter."

"I am most awfully sorry," I said. "We had a little difficulty, but got over it all right."

"What happened?" he enquired, watching me closely, and I felt myself getting red like a guilty schoolboy, for I did not particularly want to tell him of Mrs. Bellamy and Winnington's infatuation for her.

"I fancy that Winnington tried your stunt of going subconscious," I said at length. "He went very deep, and was away a long time, and I got rather worried. You see, I don't understand these things properly. And then, as he was coming back, I saw him, and took him for a ghost, and got the wind up."

"You *saw* him?" exclaimed Taverner. "How did you manage to do that? You are not clairvoyant."

"I saw a grey, spindle-shaped drift of mist, the same as we saw the time Black, the airman, nearly died."

"You saw that?" said Taverner in surprise. "Do you mean to say that Winnington took the etheric double out? How long was he subconscious?"

"About twenty-four hours."

"Good God!" cried Taverner. "The man's probably dead!"

"He's nothing of the sort," I replied. "He is alive and kicking. Kicking vigorously, in fact." I added, remembering the scene of the morning."

"I cannot conceive," said Taverner, "how the etheric double, the vehicle of the life forces, could be withdrawn for so long a time without the disintegration of the physical form commencing. Where was he, and what was he up to? Perhaps, however, he was immediately over the bed, and merely withdrew from his physical body to escape its discomfort."

"He was in the dispensary when I first saw him," I answered, devoutly hoping that Taverner would not need any further information as to Winnington's whereabouts. "He followed me back to his room and I coaxed him into his body."

Taverner gave me a queer look. "I suppose you took the preliminary precaution of making sure that it *was* Winnington you had got hold of?"

"Good Lord, Taverner, is there a possibility—?"

"Come upstairs and let us have a look at him. I can soon tell you."

Winnington was lying in a room lit only by a night-light,

151

and though he turned his head at our entrance, did not speak. Taverner went over to the bed and switched on the reading lamp standing on the bedside table. Winnington flinched at the sudden brightness, and growled something, but Taverner threw the light full into his eyes, watching them closely, and to my surprise, the pupils did not contract.

"I was afraid so," said Taverner.

"Is anything wrong?" I enquired anxiously. "He seems all right."

"Everything is wrong, my dear boy," answered Taverner. "I am sure you did the best you knew, but you did not know enough. Unless you thoroughly understand these things it is best to leave them to nature."

"But—but—he is alive," I exclaimed, bewildered.

"*It* is alive," corrected Taverner. "That is not Winnington, you know."

"Then who in the world is it? It looks like it to me."

"That we must try and find out. Who are you?" he continued, raising his voice and addressing the man on the bed.

"You know damn well," came the husky whisper.

"I am afraid I don't, answered Taverner. "I must ask you to tell me."

"Why, W—," I began, but Taverner clapped his hand over my mouth.

"Be quiet, you fool, you have done enough damage, never let it know the real name."

Then, turning back to the sick man again, he repeated his question.

"John Bellamy," came the sulky answer.

Taverner nodded and drew me out of the room.

"Bellamy?" he asked. "That is the name of the man who took the Hirschmanns' house. Has Winnington had anything to do with him?"

"Look here, Taverner," I said, "I will tell you something I had not meant to let you know. Winnington has got a

152

fixation on Bellamy's wife, and apparently he has brooded over it, and phantasied over it, till in his unconscious imagination he has substituted himself for Bellamy."

"That may quite well be, it may be an ordinary case of mental trouble; we will investigate that end of the stick by and by; but, for the present, why has Bellamy substituted himself for Winnington?"

"A wish-fulfilment," I replied. "Winnington is in love with Bellamy's wife; he wishes he were Bellamy in order to possess her, therefore his delirium expresses the subconscious wish as an actuality, the usual Freudian mechanism, you know—the dream as the wish-fulfilment."

"I dare say," answered Taverner. "The Freudians explain a lot of things they don't understand. But what about Bellamy, is he in a trance condition?"

"He is apparently quite all right, or he was, about half an hour ago. I saw him when he came down to the post with his wife. He was quite all right, and uncommon civil, in fact."

"I dare say," said Taverner drily. "You and Winnington always were chums. Now look here, Rhodes, you are not being frank with me. I must get to the bottom of this business. Now tell me all about it."

So I told him. Narrated in cold blood, it sounded the flimsiest phantasy. When I had finished, Taverner laughed.

"You have done it this time, Rhodes," he said. "And you who are so straight-laced, of all people!" and he laughed again.

"What is your explanation of the matter?" I enquired, somewhat nettled by his laughter. "I can quite understand Winnington's soul, or whatever may be the technical name for it, getting out of its body and turning up in Mrs. Bellamy's room, we have had several cases of that sort of thing; and I can quite understand Winnington's Freudian wish-fulfillment, it is the most understandable thing of the whole business; the only thing that is not clear to me is the

153

change in character of the two men; Bellamy is certainly improved, for the moment, at any rate; and Winnington is in a very bad temper and slightly delirious."

"And therein lies the crux of the whole problem. What do you suppose has happened to those two men?"

"I haven't a notion," I answered.

"But I have," said Taverner. "Narcotics, if you take enough of them, have the effect of putting you out of your body, but the margin is a narrow one between enough and too much, and if you take the latter, you go out and don't come back. Winnington found out, through you, Bellamy's weakness, and, being able to leave his body at will as a trained Initiate can, watched his chance when Bellamy was out of his body in a pipe dream, and then slipped in, obsessed him, in fact, leaving Bellamy to wander houseless. Bellamy, craving for his drug, and cut off from the physical means of gratification, scents from afar the stock we have in the dispensary, and goes there; and when he sees you with a hypoderemic syringe—for an ensouled etheric can see quite well—he instinctively follows you, and you, meddling in matters of which you know nothing, put him into Winnington's body."

As Taverner was speaking I realized that we had the true explanation of the phenomena; point by point it fitted in with all I had witnessed.

"Is there anything that can be done to put matters right?" I asked, now thoroughly chastened.

"There are several things that can be done, but it is a question as to what you would consider to be right."

"Surely there can be no doubt upon that point?—get the men sorted back into their proper bodies."

"You think that would be right?" said Taverner. "I am not so certain. In that case you would have three unhappy people; in the present case, you have two who are very happy, and one who is very angry, the world on the whole, being richer."

"But how about Mrs. Bellamy?" I said. "She is living

with a man she is not married to?"

"The law would consider her to be married to him," answered Taverner. "Our marriage laws only separate for sins of the body, they do not recognize adultery of the soul; so long as the body has been faithful, they would think no evil. A change of disposition for the worse, whether under the influence of drugs, drink, or insanity, does not constitute grounds for a divorce under our exalted code, therefore a change of personality for the better under a psychic influence does not constitute one either. The mandarins cannot have it both ways."

"Any way," I replied, "it does not seem to me moral."

"How do you define morality?" said Taverner.

"The law of the land—," I began.

"In that case a man's admission to Heaven would be decided by Act of Parliament. If you go through a form of marriage with a woman a day before a new marriage law takes effect, you will go to prison, and subsequently to hell, for bigamy; whereas, if you go through the same ceremony with the same woman the day after, you will live in the odour of sanctity and finally go to heaven. No, Rhodes, we will have to seek deeper than that for our standards."

"Then," said I, "how would you define immorality?"

"As that," said Taverner, "which retards the evolution of the group soul of the society to which one belongs. There are times when law-breaking is the highest ethical act; we can all think of such occasions in history, the many acts of conformity, both Catholic and Protestant, for example. Martyrs are law-breakers, and most of them were legally convicted at the time of their execution; it has remained for subsequent ages to canonize them."

"But to return to practical politics, Taverner, what are you going to do with Winnington?"

"Certify him," said Taverner, "and ship him off to the county asylum as soon as we can get the ambulance."

"You must do as you see fit," I replied, "but I am

155

damned if I will put my name on that certificate."

"You lack the courage of your convictions, but may I take it that you will not protest?"

"How the hell can I? I should only get certified myself."

"You must expect your good to be evil spoken of in this wicked world," rejoined my partner, and the discussion was likely to have developed into the first quarrel we had ever had when the door suddenly opened and the nurse stood there.

"Doctor," she said, "Mr. Winnington has passed away."

"Thank God!" said I.

"Good Lord!" said Taverner.

We went upstairs and stood beside that which lay upon the bed. Never before had I so clearly realized that the physical form is not the man. Here was a house that had been tenanted by two distinct entities, that had stood vacant for thirty-six hours, and that now was permanently empty. Soon the walls would crumble and the roof fall in. How could I ever have thought that this was my friend? A quarter of a mile away, the soul that had built this habitation was laughing in its sleeve, and somewhere, probably in the dispensary, a furious entity that had recently been imprisoned behind its bars was raging impotently, nosing at the stoppers of the poison bottles for the stimulants it no longer had the stomach to hold. My knees gave under me, and I dropped into a chair, nearer to fainting than I have ever been since my first operation.

"Well, that is settled, anyway," I said in a voice that sounded strange in my own ears.

"You think so? Now, I consider the trouble is just beginning," said Taverner. "Has it struck you that so long as Bellamy was imprisoned in a body, we knew where he was and could keep him under control? But now he is loose in the unseen world, and will take a considerable amount of catching."

"Then you think he will try to interfere with his wife and—and her husband?"

"What would you do if you were in his shoes?" said Taverner.

"And yet you don't consider the transaction as immoral?"

"I do not. It has done no harm to the group spirit, or the social morale, if you prefer the term. On the other hand, Winnington is running an enormous risk. Can he keep Bellamy at bay now he is out of the body? and if he cannot, what will happen? Remember Bellamy's time to die had not come, and therefore he will hang about, an earth-bound ghost, like that of a suicide; and if tuberculosis is a disease of the vital forces, as I believe it to be, how long will it be before the infected life that now ensouls it will cause the old trouble to break out in Bellamy's body? And when Bellamy the second is out on the astral plane—dead, as you call it—what will Bellamy the first have to say to him? And what will they do to Mrs. Bellamy between them, making her neighborhood their battleground?

"No, Rhodes, there is no special hell for those who dabble in forbidden things; it would be superfluous."

Recalled

"Be off with the old love e'er you're on with the new."

"How many people are there in the waiting room, Bates?" enquired Taverner of the butler at the end of a long day in the Harley Street consulting room.

"Two, sir," answered that functionary. "A lady and a gentleman."

"Ah," said Taverner. "Well show the lady in."

"I think they came together, sir."

"Then show the gentleman in. A man never brings his wife on these expeditions," he added to me. "She comes with a friend; but a man will let his wife bring him, he being the weaker sex and in need of protection where his nerves are concerned."

They arrived together, however, in spite of Taverner's instructions, and the butler announced them as Colonel and Mrs. Eustace. He was a tall, fine looking man, much bronzed by tropical suns, and she was one of those women who make one proud of one's race, slender, graceful, with the controlled fire of a thoroughbred, the fruit of many generations of refining shelter and worthy pride. They made a fine pair, such as the society papers love to picture, and they both looked perfectly healthy.

It was the wife who opened the ball.

"We, that is, my husband, wants to consult you, Dr. Taverner, about a matter which has disturbed us lately—a recurring nightmare."

Taverner bowed. The husband never spoke. I gathered that he had been dragged here against his will.

"I always know when it's coming," Mrs. Eustace continued, "because he begins to mutter in his sleep; then he speaks louder and louder, and finally he leaps up, rushes

158

across the room, and crashes into the furniture before I can do anything to stop him; and then wakes up in a dreadful state, don't you, Tony?" she demanded, turning to the silent man at her side.

Meeting with no response from him, she again took up the burden of her story.

"As soon as I realized that the nightmare was recurring regularly I took to rousing him at the first sign of disturbance, and this proved fairly effective, for it prevented the rush across the room, but we neither of us dared go to sleep again till daylight. In fact, to be frank with you doctor, I seem to be catching it."

"You also have the nightmare?" asked Taverner.

"No, not the actual nightmare, but an indefinable sense of dread, as if some dangerous enemy were threatening."

"What does your husband say when he talks in his sleep?"

"Ah, that I cannot tell you, for he speaks in one of the native dialects. I suppose I ought to learn it, ought I not, Tony? For we shall be going to India next trooping season."

"It will not be necessary," replied her husband, "for we shall not be returning to that district." His pleasant, cultured voice was in keeping with his appearance; he was a type of the administrator of empire who is fast dying out. Such men will not submit themselves to a native democracy.

Taverner fired a question at him suddenly.

"What do you dream about?" he demanded, looking him straight in the eyes. One felt the barriers go up in an instant, but he answered with the control that breeding teaches. "The usual sort of thing, bogeys, you know; want to run and can't. I ought to have left all such things behind in the nursery."

I am no psychic, but I knew that he was lying, and that he had no intention of confiding anything to anybody. He had come to Taverner in order to quiet his wife, not because he desired help. He had probably got his own ideas as to the nature of his affliction, and they were such that he did not care to voice them.

Taverner turned to the wife again. "You say that the nightmare communicates itself to you? May I ask you to detail the nature of your sensations?"

Mrs. Eustace looked at her husband and hesitated. "My husband thinks I am very imaginative," she said.

"Never mind," said Taverner, "tell me your imaginations."

"I am wide awake, of course, after—after the disturbance—and sometimes I imagine I have seen a native woman in dark blue draperies with gold sequins dangling on her forehead and many bracelets on her arms, and she seems very excited and distressed and to be trying to talk to my husband, and then when I interfere and rouse him, she tries to push me away. It is after I rouse him that I have the sense of malignancy, as if someone were trying to injure me if they could only manage it."

"I am afraid," said Colonel Eustace, "that I have thoroughly alarmed my wife."

We turned and looked at him in involuntary surprise; his voice had entirely changed its timbre. The self-control of his breed could hold the muscles of the face steady, but could not prevent that tensing of the whole frame under stress which sent the pitch of his voice up half an octave and gave a metallic edge to its tones.

"I suppose," he continued, as if anxious to distract our attention, "that you will prescribe open air and exercise; in fact that is just my own idea, and we have been thinking of going to the Kent coast for golf, so I dare say that the sooner we get off the better. There is no use in hanging about in London without a reason."

"You forget, dear," said his wife, "that I have to open the exhibition of native art on Saturday."

"Oh yes, of course," he answered hastily, "must stop over Saturday, go down on Monday."

There was a pause. The interview seemed to have come to a dead end. Mrs. Eustace looked appealing from her husband to Taverner and back again, but the one could not, and the other would not assist her. I felt that she had hoped great things of a visit to Taverner, and that, disappointed, she had no other card to play against the fate that was enveloping her. I also thought that her eyes had in them a look of apprehension.

Taverner broke the silence at last.

"If Colonel Eustace ever cares to consult me," he said, "I shall be very glad to assist him, because I think I could be of service to him."

Our unwilling patient sat up at this home thrust and opened his mouth as if to speak, but Taverner, turning to the wife, continued.

"And if Mrs. Eustace should ever be in need of my assistance, it is equally at her disposal."

"I trust there is little likelihood of that," said her husband, rising. "She is in excellent health."

And Bates opening the door in response to Taverner's ring, we bowed them out.

"An unsatisfactory blighter," I remarked as the door closed behind them.

"Not ready yet," said Taverner. "He has a few things to learn in the course of evolution, and unless I am much mistaken, he will be learning them very shortly. Then we may hear from him again. Never make the mistake of confusing unripe fruit with bad fruit."

We heard of them again, and sooner than even Taverner expected, when a couple of days later I threw across to him an evening paper which contained the announcement that Mrs. Eustace, owing to her sudden indisposition, would not be opening the exhibition of Indian Art at the Aston Galleries as announced, but that the task would be performed by some other social luminary.

"Of course it may be the flu," I said.

"Or the colic," said Taverner.

161

"Or even housemaid's knee," he added, for he was not communicative to sceptics.

The next move did not come as soon as I expected, who was looking for Colonel Eustace every time the bell rang, but in the end he appeared, and it was obvious to the most casual glance that he had been through a good deal in the interval.

The way he lay back in his chair showed that he was at the end of his tether, mental and physical, and Taverner relieved him of the effort of opening the conversation.

"How did you come to hear of me?" he asked. "I always thought my light was adequately bushelled from all except those of the same way of thinking as myself."

"My wife heard of you," was the reply. "She is interested in—in your line of work."

"Ah, she is a student of the occult?"

"I shouldn't call her a student of it," said Eustace, wriggling at the word occult. "She dabbles in it, and goes to lectures on Eastern mysticism that are no more like the real thing than—than the cat's like a tiger," he added with a sudden rush of emotion, pointing to the housekeeper's tabby that happened to be patronizing our hearthrug. "I wish to God she'd let it alone," he added wearily.

"I take it," said Taverner quietly, "that you are not a believer in the subject."

"If you had asked me that question a week ago," said Eustace, "I should have answered, no, but today—I don't know what to say. But I can tell you one thing," he cried, the banked fires blazing forth again, "if occultism isn't true, if you haven't got the powers you're credited with, then it's all up with Evelyn."

"I take it," said Taverner quietly, gathering up the control of the interview with voice and manner, "that something is affecting your wife which you guess to be of occult origin though you do not understand its method of working?"

"I understand its method of working all right," said our

162

visitor grimly, "though I had never believed such tales."

"Will you give me particulars?" said Taverner, "and then I shall be able to form an opinion."

"I may as well tell you the whole story," said Colonel Eustace, "for I don't suppose, as a man of the world, you will attach the importance to it that my wife might if she got to hear of it. Not that there is not perfect confidence between us, but women don't understand these matters, and it's no use trying to make 'em.

"You may remember that my wife, at our last interview, spoke of dreaming about a native woman and hearing an Indian dialect spoken? I think from her description, that what she saw was a vision of a woman I kept for some time when I was stationed on the Border, and who made a good deal of fuss when I sent her away, as they sometimes do. I have often heard that if a man enters into—er—relations with a native woman, they have an uncanny knack of laying hold of your soul by their heathen jiggery-spookery. I never believed it, laughed at it, in fact, when I saw another fellow bothered in the same way, but, my God, it's true. That woman has haunted my dreams ever since she died, and since I married Evelyn she has turned into an avenging devil."

"What condition is your wife in at the present moment?" enquired Taverner.

"In a stupor. The doctors talk about sleepy sickness but—" with a grim laugh. "I know better. I saw her go into the condition, and I know what it is. I tell you I heard those two women talking together, Huneefa in the broken English I taught her, as plainly as I hear you, and from that time, ten days ago, Evelyn has never recovered full consciousness and her strength is slowly ebbing away. They told me today that they did not expect her to last through the night," he added, his voice breaking, and putting up his hand to hide his twitching lips.

"Would you care for me to see your wife?" said Taverner. "It is difficult for me to advise you unless I do so."

163

"I have the car at the door to take you to her, if you will be good enough to come."

"There is one thing I must ask of you, however, before I undertake the case," said Taverner, "and that is, if, when you have heard my advice, you decide to follow it, you will go through to the end. There is nothing more disastrous than to start upon an occult undertaking and then back out of it."

"Unless you can do something, there is nothing that can be done," said Eustace brokenly, and we followed him out to the car.

I had thought Mrs. Eustace a beautiful woman when I had seen her in the formal clothes of our civilization, but lying relaxed in her white draperies on her white bed, she was more like my boyhood's idea of an angel than anything I have ever seen in picture or statuary. I could understand why her husband adored her.

I did not need the stethoscope to tell me that life was at low ebb. No pulse was perceptible in the wrist, and it was only an occasional faint stir of the laces on her bosom that showed she still breathed. There was little doubt she would not last the night; in fact she might go at any moment.

Taverner sent the nurse out of the room, and placed Eustace and myself at the far end. Then he seated himself beside the bed and gazed intently into the face of the unconscious woman, and I knew by his concentration that his mind was seeking to make contact with her soul wherever it might be. I saw him lay his hand on her breast, and guessed that he was calling her back into her body, and as I watched, I saw the inspirations deepen and become regular and the waxen passivity pass from the face.

Then she spoke, and at the sound of her voice it was all I could do to keep her husband from rushing across to her then and there.

"I am asked to tell you," came the slow, faltering words, "that the money was returned, even if it never reached you."

164

Eustace gave a groan, and dropped his head in his hands. "I am also asked to tell you," went on the faltering voice, "that it would have been a son."

Taverner lifted his hand from her breast and the breathing slowed down again and the face resumed its deathly fixation.

"Can you make anything of that?" he asked of Eustace.

"Yes," replied the man, raising his face from his hands. "It exactly confirms what I thought. It is that devil Huneefa; this is her revenge."

Taverner led us from the room.

"I want full particulars," he said. "I cannot deal with the case unless I have them."

Eustace looked uncomfortable. "I will tell you anything I can," he said at length. "What is it you want to know? The whole thing would make a long story."

"What was the origin of your affair with this Indian girl? Was she a professional courtezan or did you buy her from her parents?"

"Neither. She did a bolt and I looked after her."

"A love affair?"

"You can call it that if you like, though I don't care to remember it since—since I have learnt what love can be."

"What was the cause of your parting?"

"Well, er, you see, there was a child coming, and I couldn't stand that. Huneefa was well enough in her way, but a Eurasian brat was more than I could endure. I suppose those affairs usually end that way."

"So you sent her back to her people?"

"I couldn't very well do that, they would probably have killed her, but I gave her a good sum of money, enough to set her up in life; they don't need much to make them happy, life is pretty simple out there."

"So you gave her sufficient capital to set up on her own as a courtezan?"

"Well, er—yes, I expect that was what she would have done with it."

"There was not much else she *could* do with it, I should imagine."

"They don't think much of that out there."

"Some castes do," said Taverner quietly. "But she sent the money back to you," he continued after a pause. "What became of her after that?"

"I believe the servants said something about suicide."

"So she did not accept the alternative you offered?"

"No—er—she didn't. It's an unpleasant incident and best forgotten. I don't suppose I came out of it altogether blameless," muttered Eustace, getting up and walking about the room.

"At any rate," he continued with the air of a man who has pulled himself together, "what are we going to do about it? Huneefa apparently knew more of—er—occultism than I credited her with, and you too from all accounts, have also got a knowledge of the matter. It is East against West; who's going to win?"

"I think," said Taverner in that quiet voice of his, "that Huneefa is going to win because she has right on her side."

"But, hang it all, a native girl—they don't think anything of that out there."

"Apparently she did."

"Some of the castes are a bit straight-laced in their way, but she would have got on all right. I gave her plenty to keep her going till after the child was done with," he continued, squaring his shoulders. "Why doesn't she go for me and let Evelyn alone? Evelyn never did her any harm. I could stand it as long as she only pestered me, but this— this is a different matter."

The appearance of the nurse interrupted our colloquy.

"Mrs. Eustace has recovered consciousness," she said. "I think you had better come."

We went to the sick room, and my professional eye told me that this was the last flicker of a dying flame.

Mrs. Eustace recognized her husband as he knelt beside her, but I do not think that Taverner and I meant anything

166

to her. She looked at him with a strange expression in her face, as if she had never seen him before.

"I did not think you were like that," she said.

He seemed perplexed by her words and not to know what answer to make to them, and then she broke the silence again.

"Oh Tony," she said, "she was only fifteen."

Then we grasped the reference.

"Never mind, Dearest," whispered the man at her side. "Forget all that. What you have to do now is to get well and strong, and then we will talk it all over when you are better."

"I am not going to get better," came the quiet voice from the bed.

"Oh, yes dear, you are. Isn't she, doctor?" appealing to Taverner.

Taverner weighed his words before answering. "It is just possible," he said at length.

"I do not wish to get better," said the voice from the bed. "Everything is so—so different to what I expected. I did not think you were like that, Tony. But I suppose all men are the same."

"You mustn't take it so to heart, dear," said the man at her side brokenly. "Everybody does it out there. They have to. It's the climate. Nobody thinks anything of it."

"I do," said the voice that came from so far off. "And so would all other women if they knew. Men are wise not to tell. Women wouldn't stand it."

"But it wasn't one of *our* women, dear."

"But it was a woman, and I am a woman, and it seems to hurt me because it hurts womanhood. I can't put it plainly, but I *feel* it, I feel it as a hurt to all that is best in me."

"What are you to do with men out on frontiers?" said the man desperately. "It is the penalty of Empire."

"It is the curse of Empire," came the far-away voice. "No wonder they hate us. I always wondered why it is that

167

we can never, never make friends of them. It is because we outrage their womankind. There are some things that are never forgiven."

"Oh, don't say that, Evelyn," said the man brokenly.

"I am not saying it to you, Tony," she answered. "I love you, just as I have always loved you, but you do not understand this thing; that is the trouble. I do not blame you for taking her, but I blame you, and bitterly, for throwing her aside."

"Good Lord," said Eustace appealingly to the supporting males, "what is one to do with a woman?"

"And she does not blame you" continued the voice, "for taking her, or for throwing her aside. She loved you and she understood. In fact she never expected anything else, she tells me. It is herself that she blames, and she has not been angry with you, but has been imploring you to help her out, to undo the wrong that has been done."

"What is it she wants? I'll do anything on earth if she will let you alone."

"She says—" the voice seemed a very long way off, like a trunk call on a telephone, "that the soul that was to have come into life through you and her was a very lofty soul indeed, a Mahatma, she called him. What is a Mahatma?"

"One of those people who stir up trouble. Never mind about him. Go on. What does she want me to do?"

"She says that, because of her attainments in the past, she was chosen to give him birth, and because he had to reconcile East and West, East and West had to be reconciled in him. Also, he had to come through a great love. I am glad it was a great love, Tony. That seems to sanctify it and to make it better somehow."

Eustace turned appalled eyes upon us.

"And because it was a great privilege, it had to be bought by a great sacrifice; she had to give up the love before she brought him to birth. I suppose that is always the way. She says they offered her a choice—she might have the love of a man of her own people, a home, and happiness; or she might have the love of a Western man for a short time, in order that the great Reconciler might come into life, and she chose the latter. She knew what it would mean when she entered on it, she said, but she found it harder than she thought. It was because you sent her so much money that she killed herself, for she knew your conscience would be at ease after that, and she did not wish you to be at ease."

"God knows, I'm not," groaned the man. "She is having her revenge all right. What more does she want, the little devil?"

"It is the Mahatma soul she is troubled about," came the answer, "and because of it she cannot rest."

"What does she want me to do?" asked the man.

"She wants us to take it."

"But, Good Lord. What does she mean? A half caste? You—Evelyn. A nigger? Oh Heavens, no, nothing doing. I would sooner have you dead than that. Let her take her twice damned Mahatma and go to whatever hell they belong to."

"No she doesn't mean that, Tony, she means that she wishes us, you and I, to take him."

"Oh well, if we can find the kid, yes; anything if only you'll get well. I'll send him to Eton and Oxford or Lhassa or Mecca, or anywhere else they have a fancy for, if they will only let you alone."

"I don't want to get well," came the voice from the depth of the pillows.

"But, dear—for my sake—you said you still loved me."

"I don't want to get well, but I suppose I must, just as she ought to have gone on living, although she did not want to because of *Him*."

"Whom?"

"The soul that was to have come, the soul who will come now, The Reconciler."

There was a pause. Then she spoke again, and her voice seemed to gain strength with each sentence.

169

"It will be very difficult, Tony."

"We'll manage somehow, dear, as long as we have each other."

"It will be more difficult than you think."

Mrs. Eustace recovered rapidly, and her husband's joy knew no bounds. He attributed it all to Taverner, though as a matter of fact, Taverner had been nothing but an onlooker as the strange drama of life and death worked itself out. As such a man will, who lives upon the surface of things and prides himself upon his matter-of-factness, Eustace soon forgot the inner aspect of the whole affair. His wife had had sleepy sickness, and thank God, was over it, therefore he rejoiced, and had much to rejoice in. For firstly, promotion had come his way, and from the command of a regiment, he had passed to one of the most important administrative posts over the heads of many seniors. Likewise, by the unexpected death of a cousin, he had become heir presumptive to a great name. And thirdly, to crown his joy, it was apparent that the name would not end with him.

We went to dinner with them on the eve of their sailing. Eustace was in the seventh heaven, with telegrams of congratulations arriving all through the meal. The face of his wife had never lost its look of remoteness and stillness, which she had brought back from her sojourn on other planes, but there was no joy in her eyes, save pleasure at his pleasure, and a rather sad smile, as of one who watched a beloved child set its heart upon a bauble.

We heard no more of them till chance gossip gave us news.

"Have you heard about the Eustaces," said a man at my club. "General Eustace, he is now. Their child, it's as black as a coal. Everybody wonders what he is going to do about it. It would probably have meant his resignation if he had not had such terrific influence with all that seditionist crowd that no one else can manage. Can't understand his being such a success with them, not much tact, and less understanding. Still they seem to hit it off. Pity about her, isn't it? An awfully nice woman. Sort of stained glass window saint. Can't understand it at all."

Some years later the Eustaces appeared on the scene again. He was now a baronet, having succeeded to his cousin's title, and he was likewise something very lofty in the Government of India, but he was also a changed man. His hair was as white as snow, and his face preternaturally aged with its deep lines and sunken eyes. Strangely enough, Lady Eustace, as she was now, had changed least of all, save that she was etherealized till she no longer seemed to be of this earth. I gathered that she led a very retired life, taking no part in the social activities that usually fall to the lot of a woman in her position.

With them was a child of five, with jet black hair, dark olive skin, slender limbs, and a pair of eyes as blue as the sea. They were the strangest eyes I have ever seen in the face of a child, for they had the depth of the sea as well as its blueness, these eyes of the West in the face of the East. I wondered what the soul would see, that looked at its native East through Western eyes.

Eustace drew me aside; he seemed to need to unbosom his soul to someone who knew the story. Pointing to the child with its mother, he said.

"You can guess what that meant to us, in our position, eh?"

"I wouldn't mind for myself," he continued, "but it's so hard for her. A crucifixion," he added.

I heard the mother's voice speaking to Taverner.

"You see it too?" she was saying softly. "Isn't it wonderful? What have I, I of all women, done to deserve such a thing?"

Then turning to the child she said: "Do you know who this gentleman is, darling?"

"Yes," said the child. "He is also One of Us, as I told you."

171

"Queer little cuss," said the father patting his son's head. "Have you found another of your friends?"

The Sea Lure

"Do you know anything about stigmata?" said my *vis-a-vis.*

It was a very unexpected question to have shot at one under the circumstances. I had been unable to evade an invitation to spend the evening with an old fellow-student who since the war had held the uninspiring post of medical officer at a poor law institution, a post for which I should say he was admirably fitted, and I now found myself facing him across a not very elegant supper table in his quarters in a great fortress of dingy red brick which looked out for miles over the grey wastes of sordidness which are South London.

I was so taken by surprise that he had to repeat his question before I answered it.

"Do you know anything about stigmata? Hysterical stigmata?" he said again.

"I have seen simulated tumours," I said, "they are fairly common, but I have never seen actual flesh wounds, such as the saints were supposed to have had."

"What do you attribute them to?" asked my companion.

"Auto-suggestion," I replied. "Imagination so vivid that it actually affects the tissues of the body."

"I have got a case in one of my wards that I should like to show you," he said. "A most curious case. I think it is hysterical stigmata; I cannot account for it any other way. A girl was brought in here a couple of days ago suffering from a gunshot wound in the shoulder. She came here to have the bullet removed, but would give no account as to how she came by the injury. We admitted her, but couldn't see any bullet, which was rather puzzling. She was in a condition of semi-stupor, which we naturally attributed to loss of blood, and so we kept her here. Of course there is nothing odd in all that, save our failure to locate the bullet, but then such things happen even with the best apparatus, and ours is a long way from being that. But here is the queer part of the case. I was sitting quietly up here last night between eleven and twelve when I heard a shriek; of course there is nothing odd about that either, in this district. But in a minute or two they rang up on the house telephone to say that I was wanted in the wards, and I went down to find this girl with *another* bullet wound. No one had heard a shot fired, all the windows were intact, there was a nurse not ten feet from her. When we X-rayed her we again failed to find the bullet, yet there was a clean hole drilled in her shoulder, and, oddest of all, it never bled a drop. What do you make of it?"

"If you are certain there is no external agency at work, then the only hypothesis is an internal one. Is she an hysterical type?"

"Distinctly. Looks as if she came out of one of Burne-Jones's pictures. Moreover, she has been in a sort of stupor each night for an hour or more at a time. It was while in this state that she developed the second wound. Would you care to come down and have a look at her? I should like to have your opinion. I know you have gone in for psychoanalysis and all sorts of things that are beyond my ken."

I accompanied him to the wards, and there we found in one of the rough infirmary beds a girl who, lying on the coarse pillow, with closed eyes and parted lips, looked exactly like the *Beata Beatrix* of Rossetti's vision, save that honey-coloured hair flowed over the pillow like seaweed. When she opened her eyes at our presence, they were green as sea-water seen from a rock.

All was quiet in the ward, for infirmary patients are settled for the night at an early hour, and my friend signed to the nurse to put screens round the bed that we might examine our case without disturbing them. It was as he had said, two obvious bullet wounds, one more recent than the other, and from their position and proximity, I judged that they have been inflicted with intention to disable, but not to kill. In fact she had been very neatly "winged" by an expert marksman. It was only the circumstances of the second shot that gave the case any interest except a criminal one.

I sat down on a chair at the bedside, and began to talk to her, seeking to win her confidence. She gazed back at me dreamily with her strange sea-green eyes and answered my questions readily enough. She seemed curiously detached, curiously indifferent to our opinion of her; as if she lived in a far-away world of her own, about which she was quite willing to talk to any one who was interested.

"Do you dream much?" I said, making the usual opening.

This seemed to touch a subject of interest.

"Oh, yes," she replied, "I dream a tremendous lot. I always have dreamt, ever since I can remember. I think my dreams are the realest part of my life—and the best part," she added with a smile, "so why shouldn't I?"

"Your dreams seem to have led you into danger recently," I answered, drawing a bow at a venture.

She looked at me sharply, as if to see how much I knew, and then said thoughtfully:

"Yes, I mustn't go there again. But I expect I shall, all the same," she added with an elfish smile.

"Can you go where you choose in your dreams?" I asked.

"Sometimes," she replied, and was about to say more, when she caught sight of my companion's bewildered face and the words died on her lips. I saw that she was what Taverner would have called "One of Us," and my interest was roused. I pitied the refined, artistic-looking girl in these sordid surroundings, her great shining eyes looking out like those of a caged creature behind bars, and I said:

"What is your work?"

"Shop girl," she replied; a smile curling the corners of her lips. "Drapery, to be precise." Her words and manner were so at variance with her description of herself, that I was still further intrigued.

"Where are you going when you come out of here?" I enquired.

She looked wearily out into distance, the little smile still hovering about her mouth.

"Back into my dreams, I expect," she replied. "I don't suppose I shall find anywhere else to go."

I knew well Taverner's generosity with necessitous cases, especially if they were of "his own kind," and I felt sure that he would be interested both in the personality of the girl and in her peculiar injuries, and I said:

"How would you like to go down to a convalescent home at Hindhead when you leave here?"

She gazed at me in silence for a moment with her strange gleaming eyes.

"Hindhead?" she asked. "What sort of a place is that?"

"It is moorland," I replied. "Heather and pine, you know, very bracing."

"Oh, if it could only be the sea!" she exclaimed wistfully. "A rocky coast, miles from anywhere, where the Atlantic rollers come in and the seabirds are flying and calling. If it could only be the sea I should get right! The moors are not my place, it is the sea I need, it is life to me."

She paused abruptly, as if she feared to have said too much, and then she added: "Please don't think that I am ungrateful, a rest and change would be a great help. Yes, I should be very thankful for a letter for the nursing home—" Her voice trailed into silence and her eyes, looking more like deep-sea water than ever, gazed unseeing into a distance where I have no doubt the gulls were flying and calling and the Atlantic rollers coming in from the West.

"She has gone off again," said my host. "It is apparently her regular time for going into a state of coma."

176

As we watched her, she took a deep inspiration, and then all breathing ceased. It ceased for so long, although the pulse continued vigorously, that I was just on the point of suggesting artificial respiration, when with a profound exhalation, the lungs took up their work with deep rhythmical gasps. Now if you observe a person's respiration closely, you will invariably find that you yourself begin to breathe with the same rhythm. It was a very peculiar rhythm which I found myself assuming, and yet it was not unfamiliar. I had breathed with that rhythm before, and I searched my subconscious mind for the clue. Suddenly I found it. It was the respiration of breathing in rough water. No doubt the cessation of breathing represented the dive. The girl was dreaming of her sea.

So absorbed was I in the problem that I would have sat up all night in the hope of finding some evidence of the mysterious assailant, but my host touched my sleeve.

"We had better be moving," he said. "Matron, you know." And I followed him out of the darkened ward.

"What do you make of it?" he enquired eagerly as soon as we were out in the corridor.

"I think as you do," I answered; "that we are dealing with a case of stigmata, but it will require more plumbing than I could give it this evening, and I should like to keep in touch with her if you are willing."

He was only too willing, seeing himself in print in the *Lancet* and possessed of that dubious type of glory which comes to the owners of curios. It was a blessed break in the monotony of his routine, and he naturally welcomed it.

Now that which is to follow will doubtless be set down as the grossest kind of coincidence, and as several such coincidences have been reported in these chronicles, I do not suppose I have much reputation for veracity anyway. But Taverner always held that some coincidences, especially those which might be conceived to serve the purpose of an intelligent Providence, were not as fortuitous as they appeared to be, but were due to causes which operated invisibly upon the subtler planes of existence, and whose effects alone were seen in our material world; and that those of us who are in touch with the unseen, as he was, and as I, to a lesser degree on account of my association with him in his work, had also come to be, might get ourselves into the hidden currents of that realm, and thereby be brought in touch with those engaged in similar pursuits. I had too often watched Taverner picking up people apparently at random and arriving at the psychological moment apparently by chance, to doubt the operation of some such laws as he described, though I neither understand their workings nor recognize them at the time; it is only in perspective that one sees the Unseen Hand.

Therefore it was that when, on my return to Hindhead, Taverner requested me to undertake a certain task, I concluded that my plans with regard to the study of the stigmata case must be set aside, and banished the matter from my mind.

"Rhodes," he said, "I want you to undertake a piece of work for me. I would go myself, but it is extremely difficult for me to get away, and you know enough of my methods by now, combined with your native common sense (in which I have much more faith than in many people's psychism) to be able to report the matter, and possibly deal with it under my instruction."

He handed me a letter. It was inscribed, "Care G.H. Frater," and began without any further preamble: "That of which you warned me has occurred. I have indeed got in out of my depth, and unless you can pull me out I shall be a drowned man, literally as well as metaphorically. I cannot get away from here and come to you; can you possibly come to me?" And a quotation from Virgil, which seemed to have little bearing on the subject, closed the appeal.

Scenting adventure, I readily acceded to Taverner's request. It was a long journey I had to undertake, and when the train came to rest at its terminus in the grey twilight of a winter afternoon, I could smell the keen salt tang of the wind that drove straight in from the West. To me there is always something thrilling in arriving at a seaside place and getting the first glimpse of the sea, and my mind reverted to that other solitary soul who had loved blue water, the girl with the Rossetti face, who lay in the rough infirmary bed in the dreary desert of South London.

She was vividly present to my mind as I entered the musty four-wheeler, which was all that the station could produce in the off-season, and drove through deserted and wind-swept streets on to the sea-front. The line of breakers showed grey through the gathering darkness as we left the asphalt and boarding houses behind us and followed the coast road out into the alluvial flats beyond the town. Presently the road began to wind upwards towards the cliffs, and I could hear the horse wheezing with the ascent, till a hail from the darkness put a stop to our progress; a figure clad in an Inverness cape appeared in the light of the carriage lamps, and a voice, which had that indefinable something which Oxford always gives a man, greeted me by name and invited me to alight.

Although I could see no sign of a habitation, I did as I was bidden, and the cabman, manoeuvring his vehicle, departed into the windy darkness and left me alone with my invisible host. He possessed himself of my bag, and we set off straight for the edge of the cliff, so far as I could make out, leaning up against the force of the gale. An invisible surf crashed and roared below us, and it seemed to me that drowning was the order of the day for both of us.

Presently, however, I felt a path under my feet.

"Keep close to the rock," shouted my guide. (Next day I knew why). And we dipped over the edge of the cliff and began to descend its face. We continued in this way for what seemed to me an immense distance—I learnt later it was about a quarter of a mile—and then, to my amazement, I heard the click of a latch. It was too dark to see anything, but warm air smote my face, and I knew that I was under cover. I heard my host fumbling with a box of matches, and as the light flared, I saw that I was in a good-sized room, apparently hewn out of the cliff face, and a most comfortable apartment. Book-lined, warmly curtained, Persian rugs on the smooth stone of the floor, and a fire of driftwood burning on the open hearth, which the toe of my companion's boot soon stirred to a blaze. The amazing contrast to my gloomy and perilous arrival took my breath away.

My host smiled. "I am afraid," he said, "that you were making up your mind to be murdered. I ought to have explained to you the nature of my habitation. I am so used to it myself, that it does not seem to me that it may appear strange to others. It is an old smuggler's lair that I have adapted to my use, and being made of the living rock, it has peculiar advantages for the work on which I am engaged."

We sat down to the meal that was already upon the table, and I had an opportunity to study the appearance of my host. Whether he was an elderly man who had preserved his youth, or a young man prematurely aged, I could not tell, but the maturity of his mind was such that I inclined to the former hypothesis, for a wide experience of men and things must have gone to the ripening of such a nature as his.

His face had something of the lawyer about it, but his hands were those of an artist. It was a combination I had often seen before in Taverner's friends, for the intellectual who has a touch of the mystic generally ends in occultism. His hair was nearly white, in strange contrast to his wind-tanned face and dark sparkling eyes. His figure was spare and athletic, and well above middle height, but his movements had not the ease of youth, but rather the measured dignity of a man who is accustomed to public appearances. It was an interesting and impressive personality, but he showed none of the signs of distress that his letter had led me to expect.

After-dinner pipes soon led to confidences, and after

sitting for a while in the warm fire-lit silence, my host seemed to gather his resolution together, and after crossing and uncrossing his legs several times uneasily, finally said:

"Well, doctor, this visit is on business, not pleasure, so we may as well 'Cut the cackle and come to the 'osse's. I suppose I appear to you to be sane enough at the present moment?"

I bowed my assent.

"At eleven o'clock you will have the pleasure of seeing me go off my head."

"Will you tell me what you are experiencing?" I said.

"You are not one of us," he replied (I had probably failed to acknowledge some sign) "but you must be in Taverner's confidence or he would not have sent you. I am going to speak freely to you. You are willing to admit, I presume, that there is more in heaven and earth than you are taught in the medical schools?"

"No one can look life honestly in the face without admitting that," I replied. "I have respect for the unseen, though I don't pretend to understand it."

"Good man" was the reply. "You will be more use to me than a brother occultist who might encourage me in my delusions. I want facts, not phantasies. Once I am certain that I am deluded, I can pull myself together; it is the uncertainty that is baffling me."

He looked at his watch; paused, and then with an effort plunged *in medias res.*

"I have been studying the elemental forces: I suppose you know what that means? The semi-intelligent entities behind the potencies of nature. We divide them into four classes—earth, air, fire and water. Now I am of the earth, earthy."

I raised my eyebrows in query, for his appearance belied the description he gave of himself.

He smiled. "I did not say of the flesh, fleshly. That is quite a different matter. But in my horoscope I have five planets in earth signs, and consequently my nature is

181

bound up with the formal side of things. Now in order to counteract this state of affairs I set myself to get in touch with the fluidic side of nature, elemental water. I have succeeded in doing so." He paused and packed the tobacco in his pipe with a nervous gesture. "But not only have I got in touch with the water elementals, but they have got in touch with me. One in particular." The pipe again required attention.

"It was a most extraordinary, exhilarating experience. Everything I lacked seemed to be added to me. I was complete, vital, in circuit with the cosmic forces. In fact, I got everything I had sought in marriage and failed to find. But, and here's the rub, the creature that called me was in the water, and it was in the water that I had to meet her. Round this headland the tides run like fury, no swimmer could hold his own against them, even in calm weather; but by night, and in a storm, which is the time she generally comes, it would be certain death; but she calls me, and she *wills* me to go to her, and one of these nights I shall do so. That is my trouble."

He stopped, but I could see by the working of his face that there was more to come so I kept silence.

He bent down and took from the side of the hearth an object which he handed to me. It was a small crucible, and had evidently been used to melt down silver.

"You will laugh when I tell you what I used that for. To make silver bullets—silver bullets to shoot with." He hid his face in his hands. "Oh, my God, I tried to murder her!" The flood-gates of emotion were open, and I could see his shoulders heave to the tide of it.

"I could see her as she swam in the moonlight, and as her shoulder rose to the stroke, I shot her in the round white curve of it, white as foam against the black water. And she vanished. Then I thought I had killed the thing I loved. I would have given heaven and earth to bring her back and to swim out there to her in the tide-race and drown with her. I was like a madman; I wandered on the shore for

182

days, I could neither eat nor sleep. And then she came again, and I knew that it was my life or hers, and I, being of the earth, clung to the life of form, and I shot her again. And now I am in torment. I love her, I long for her, I call to her in the unseen, and when she comes to me, I wait for her with a rifle."

He came to an abrupt stop and remained rigid, gazing into the heart of the dying fire, his empty pipe in his hand. I glanced surreptitiously at my watch, and saw that the hands were pointing to eleven. His hour was upon him.

He rose, and crossing the room, drew back the draperies at the far end and revealed a casement window. Flinging it open, he seated himself on the sill and gazed fixedly into the darknesss without. Moving softly I took my place behind him, where I could see what was happening outside, and be ready to seize hold of him if necessary.

For a while we waited; the clouds hurried over the moon sometimes letting its radiance pour out in a silver flood, but more often hiding its face and leaving us in the roaring, crashing darkness of that surf-beaten coast.

It was indeed a "magic casement opening on the foam of perilous seas in faery lands forlorn." I shall never forget that vigil. Nothing but heaving waters as far as eye could see, all flecked with foam in the moonlight where the reefs were hidden by the flood tide, which swirled below us like a mill-race. My companion's fine-cut features had the boldness and immobility of the statue of a Roman emperor, silhouetted against the silver background of the water.

He never stirred, he might have been carven in stone, till I saw a quiver run through him and knew that he had found that for which he waited. I strained my eyes to see what it was that had caught his attention, and sure enough, right out in the track of the moonlight, something was swimming. Coming steadily towards us through the reefs, the white shoulder lifting to the stroke just as he had described it, nearer, nearer, where no living soul could have swum in that wild tide-race, till, not thirty yards from the base of the cliffs, I could descry a woman's form with the hair streaming out like seaweed.

The man at the window leant right out stretching forth his arms to the swimmer, and I, fearing that he would overbalance, put mine gently round him and drew him back into the room. He seemed oblivious of my presence, and yielded to the pressure as if asleep, and I lowered him gently to the floor where he lay motionless in a trance. I stooped to feel his pulse, and as I counted the slow beats, I heard a sound that made me hold my breath and listen. It seemed as if the sea had risen and filled the room, and yet not the material sea, but its ghost; shadowy impalpable sea-water flowed in waves to the very ceiling, and the sea-creatures looked in from without.

Then I saw the form of a woman at the window. Shining with its own luminosity, it was clearly visible in the green gloom that was like the bottom of the sea. The hair floated out like seaweed, the shoulders gleamed like marble, the face was that of a *Beata Beatrix* awakened from her dream, and the eyes were like sea-water seen from a rock, and there, sure enough, were the marks where the silver bullets had wounded her.

We looked into each other's eyes, and I am convinced she saw me as clearly as I saw her, and that she knew me, for the same faint smile that I had seen before hovered on her lips. I spoke as one addressing a sentient creature.

"Do not try to take him in this way," I said, "or you will kill him. Trust me, I will make things right. I will explain everything."

She looked at me with those strange sea-green eyes of hers, as if piercing my very soul; apparently satisfied, she withdrew, and the shadowy sea-water flowed after till the room was emptied.

I came to myself to find the quizzical eyes of my host fixed on me as he sat in his chair smoking his pipe.

"Physician, heal thyself!" he said.

I rose stiffly from my seat and subsided into a chair,

lighting a cigarette with numbed fingers. A few whiffs of the soothing smoke steadied my nerves and enabled me to think.

"Well, doctor," came the voice of my host in gentle raillery, "what is your diagnosis?"

I paused, for I realized the critical nature of that which I was about to do.

"If I were to tell you that last night I was at the bedside of that girl we saw swimming out there, and that she had two bullet-wounds in her shoulder, what would you say?"

He leant forward, his lips parted, but no sound came from them.

"If I told you that the bullet-wounds arose spontaneously without any external agency, and that the doctor considered them to be hysterical stigmata, how would you explain it?"

"By Jove," he exclaimed, "it sounds like a case of repercussion! I came across several instances of it when I was studying the Scottish State Papers relating to the witch trials in the sixteenth century. It was a thing often related of the witches, that they could project the astral double out of the physical body and so appear at a distance. I had something of that kind at the back of my mind when I made the silver bullets. Old country-folk believe that it is only with silver bullets that you can shoot a witch. Lead has no effect on them. But you mean to tell me that you have actually seen—seen in the flesh—the woman whose astral body it was we saw out there in the water? Good Lord, doctor, I am indeed out of my depth! I don't believe I ever thought in my heart that the things I was studying were real, I thought they were just states of consciousness."

"But aren't states of consciousness real?"

"Yes, of course they are, on their own plane, that is the whole teaching of occult science. But I always thought they were entirely subjective, experiences of the imagination. It never occurred to me that anyone else could share them."

185

"You—we both—seem to have shared in this girl's dreams, for she escapes from her dreary reality by imagining herself swimming in the sea."

"Tell me about her—What is she like? Where did you meet her?"

"Before I answer that question, will you first tell me your motive for asking it? Do you want to be rid of her? Because if so, I can probably persuade her to leave you alone."

"I want to make her acquaintance," came the reluctant reply. "I was pretty badly bitten once, and haven't spoken to a woman for years, but this—seems to be different. Yes, I would like to make her acquaintance. Tell me, who is she? What is she? What is her name? What are her people like?"

"She is, as you have seen, of very unusual appearance. Many people would not consider her beautiful, others would rave about her. She is somewhere in the twenties. Intelligent, refined, her voice is that of an educated woman. Her name I do not know, for she was lying in an infirmary bed, and was therefore just a number. Nor do I know what her people are. I don't fancy she has any, for I gathered she was entirely destitute. She is a shop girl by trade—drapery, to be precise."

During this recital my host's face had changed in an indefinable way. The cheeks had fallen in, the eyes had lost their brilliancy and become sunken, and a network of lines sprang up all over the skin. He had suddenly become worn and old, the burnt-out cinder of a man. I was at a loss to account for this appalling change till his words gave me the clue.

"I think," he said in a voice that had lost all resonance, "that I had better let the matter drop. A shop girl, you say? No, it would be most unsuitable, most unwise. It never does to marry outside one's own class. I—er—No, we will say no more about the matter. I must pull myself together. Now that I understand the condition I am sure I

186

have the will-power to return to the normal. In fact I feel that you have cured me already. I am sure that I shall never have a return of my dream, its power over me is broken. If you will give me your companionship for just a few more days till I feel that my health is quite reestablished I shall be all right. But we will not refer to the matter again; I beg of you, doctor, not to refer to it, for I wish to banish the whole experience from my mind."

Looking at him as he crouched in his chair, the broken, devitalized wreck of the man whose fine presence I had admired, it seemed to me that the remedy was worse than the disease. He had, by an effort of his trained will, broken the subtle magnetic rapport that bound him to the girl, and with the breaking of it, the source of his vitality had gone.

"But look here," I protested, "are you sure that you are doing the right thing? The girl may be quite all right in herself, even if she has to work for a living. If she means all this to you, surely you are throwing away something big."

For answer he rose, and going silently out of the room, closed the door behind him, and I knew that argument was useless. He was bound within his limitations and unable to escape out of them into the freedom which is life. Of the earth, earthy.

I wrote a full account of these transactions to Taverner, and then settled down to await his instructions as to future procedure. The situation was somewhat strained. My host looked like a man whose life had fallen about his ears. Day by day, almost hour by hour, he seemed to age. He sat in his rock-hewn room, refusing to move, and it was with the greatest difficulty that I succeeded in coaxing him out daily for a walk on the smooth hard sands that stretched for miles when the tide receded. When the water was up he would not go near it; he seemed to have a horror of the sea.

Two days passed in this way, with no word from Taverner, till on our return from our morning walk, we found that a slip of paper had been pushed under the door of our

187

cavern. It was the ordinary post office intimation to say that a telegram had been brought in our absence, and now awaited me at the post office. Not sorry for a break in our routine, though a little uneasy about my patient, I immediately set off on the three mile walk to the town to get my telegram. I went up the perilous path cut out of the face of the rock, and then along the cliff road, for though it was possible to walk into town on the sands, the tide was coming in, and it was doubtful if I would be able to round the headland before the undercliff was awash; at any rate my host thought it was too risky for a stranger to attempt.

As I went up over the turf of the headland, a thrill ran through me like wine to a starving man. The air was full of dancing golden motes; the turf, the rock, the sea, were alive with a vast life and I could feel their slow breathing. And I thought of the man I had left in the dwelling in the cliff face, the man who had come so far in his quest of the larger life, but who dared not take the final step.

At the post office of that desolate and forsaken watering-place I duly received my telegram.

"Am sending stigmata case. She arrives 4:15. Arrange lodgings and meet her. Taverner."

I gave a whistle that brought the postmaster and his entire staff to the front counter, and taking counsel with them, I obtained certain addresses whither I repaired, and finally succeeded in arranging suitable accommodation. What the upshot would be I could not imagine, but at any rate it was out of my hands now.

At the appointed time I presented myself at the station and soon picked out my protegee from the scanty handful of arrivals. She looked very tired with the journey; frail, forlorn, and shabby. What with the fume of the engine and the frowst of the cab, there was no smell of the sea to revive her, and I could hardly get a word out of her during the drive to the lodgings, but as she disembarked from the

188

crazy vehicle, a rush of salt-laden wind struck her in the face, and below us, in the dusk, we heard the crash-rush of the waves on the pebbles. The effect was magical. The girl flung up her head like a startled horse, and vitality seemed to flow into her, and when I presented her to her landlady, there was little to indicate the convalescent I had represented her to be.

When I returned to the rock-hewn eyrie of my host, his courtesy forbade him to question me as to the cause of my long absence, and indeed, I doubt if he felt any interest, for he seemed to have sunk into himself so completely that his grip on life was gone. I could hardly rouse him sufficiently to make him take the evening paper I had brought from the town; it lay on his knee unread while he gazed into the driftwood fire with unseeing eyes.

The following day the tide had not receded sufficiently for a morning walk, so it was not till the afternoon that we went for our constitutional. We had left it rather late, and on our way back in the early winter twilight we had to ford several gathering pools. We swung along over the sand barefoot, boots slung over our shoulders and trousers rolled to the knee, for it was one of those mild days that often come in January—when out on the edge of the incoming surf we saw a figure.

"Good Lord!" said my companion. "Who in the world is the fool out there? He will be cut off by the tide and won't be able to get out of the bay by now. He will have to come up by the cliff path. I had better warn him." And he let out a halloo.

But the wind was blowing towards us, and the figure, out there in the noise of the surf, did not hear. My companion went striding over the sand towards the solitary wader, but I, who had somewhat better eyes than he had, did not elect to accompany him, for I had seen long hair blown out like seaweed and the flying folds of a skirt.

I saw him walk into the ankle-deep water that creamed over the flat sands, forerunner of the advancing line of breakers. He called again to the wader, who turned but did not come towards him, but instead held out her hand with a strange welcoming gesture. Slowly, as if fascinated by that summoning hand, he advanced into the water, till he was within touch of her. The first of the advancing waves smote her knees and ran past her in yeasty foam. The next smote her hip; the tide was rising fast with the wind behind it. A shower of over-carried spray hit him in the face. Still the girl would not move, and the waves were mounting up perilously behind her. It was not until he caught the outstretched hand that she yielded and let him draw her ashore.

They came towards me over the sand, still hand in hand, for they had forgotten to loosen their fingers, and I saw that the life had come back to his face and that his eyes sparkled with the brilliancy of fire. I drew back into the shadow of a rock, and oblivious of me, they passed up the steep path to the cliff dwelling. A glow of firelight shone as he opened the door to admit her, and I saw her wet hair streaming over her shoulders like seaweed and his profile was like the rock-cut statue of a Roman emperor.

The Power House

I had been dragged at Taverner's chariot-wheels all down Charing Cross Road in quest of some tome that caused the merchants of that district to eye us askance. Finally he gave up the quest in despair, and as a reward for my patience, promised me tea in a cafe the walls whereof were decorated with particularly choice devils. My fleshly soul yearned for a brand of oyster cocktail which may be obtained at the corner of Tottenham Court Road, but Taverner, who was fond of tea as an old maid, had so evidently set his heart on the devil-shop that I sacrificed my well-being to his desires.

New Oxford Street ceases to be respectable to the east of Charing Cross Road, and becomes shabby-genteel and dubious until the plain commerciality of Holborn restores it to self-respect. The side turnings are narrow and lead to Bohemia; delicatessen shops and emporiums of haberdashery of an amazing brilliance and instability loom in their narrow canyons; strange faces look from the windows of their cliff-like facades. It is all un-English, sordid, and vaguely sinister. The crust over the underworld is thin here.

On an island in the midst of that roaring torrent of traffic we were compelled to halt. A bare-headed, sleek-haired woman jammed a marketing basket into the small of my back, and the yard of bread protruding from it prodded Taverner, under whose elbow peered out the pallid sharp-featured face of a little "matcher" whose bunch of patterns was clutched in a small red fist as if life itself depended on them. Past us roared the tide of commercial London, and through that tide there darted another flotsam of the traffic, to be cast up as if by a breaker upon our island. My mind instantly reverted to my school-book pictures of Richard III, the same ferrety, yet intellectual face, low stature, and slightly hunched back which served to barrel out the chest into an enormously powerful though ungainly structure. The greyness of the skin told of chronic ill-health, or an unwholesome life in the foul and sunless air of which the denizens of that district are so fond. The eyes were a pale grey, and of a brightness and beadiness usually associated with black eyes of the boot-button type. The mouth, large and thin-lipped, looked cruel, the mouth of the cold sensualist, who has sensations but no emotions.

The face caught my attention even in that brief glance, for it was a face of power, but his subsequent behaviour fixed all details in my mind, for no sooner had he raised his eyes to meet Taverner's than his expression changed from that of an alert jackdaw to a cornered cat. He emitted a sound that was almost like a hiss, and darted straight back into the stream of traffic from which he had emerged.

A yell, a crash, and a shriek of brakes showed that the expected had happened, and at our very feet the man lay insensible, blood pouring from a cut in his head where it had hit the curb. Almost before the car that struck him had backed away, Taverner and I were bending over him; I examining his head, and Taverner, to my intense surprise, examining his pockets. He withdrew a shabby and bulging notebook from the breast pocket, glanced hastily through it, seemed to register mental notes in that miraculous memory of his, and returned it whence he had taken it, and by the time the white-faced chauffeur was beside us, had resumed his most professional manner and was rendering first aid in the orthodox fashion. A policeman's helmet loomed through the traffic, and Taverner twitched my sleeve, and we, in our turn, made a bolt through the congested mass of vehicles, and with better luck than the ferret-faced man, reached the pavement in safety, and slipped down a side street that led to Taverner's abode of

192

the devils, leaving it to those who enjoy such things to superintend the embarkation of the casualty in its ambulance.

"That is an amazing piece of luck," said Taverner. "Do you know who that was? It was Josephus. He is supposed to be in Tunisia, even Paris had got too hot for him, and here he is, back in London, and looking prosperous too, so he must be in mischief, and I've got his address."

I could not join in Taverner's enthusiasm over the discovery of Josephus, as I had not the pleasure of that worthy's acquaintance, and Taverner was soon engaged in revelry over hot buttered toast and much too interested in the symbolism of the devils careering round the frieze to attend to anything so mundane; meanwhile I endeavoured to twine my legs around the rungs of the little tile-topped table designed for the accommodation of the under-nourished breed that feeds at such places. Taverner disposed of his long legs by stretching them across the gangway, and between us I am afraid we took up much more than our fair share of the exiguous accommodation.

Luckily we had the place practically to ourselves, for the tea hour was overpast, and there was no one to note the intrusion of the Philistines upon this West Central Bohemia save a man and woman lingering over the remains of their meal at a neighbouring table, and they were much too absorbed in their conversation to pay any attention to anything save their own affairs.

Or rather, to be strictly accurate, the man was absorbed, for the woman seemed to be listening wearily, with an air of uneasy detachment, as if seeking an opportunity to put an end to the interview and make her escape from the importunity of her companion. I could see her face across the dimly lit room, its expressionless calm in strange contrast to the tenseness of the man who spoke to her; the large grey eyes, set in the pallor of an oval face, seemed to be gazing at some far horizon, oblivious of the narrow Bloomsbury streets.

Oblivious, that was the word to characterize her. She was oblivious of her companion, his viewpoint, his needs; her eyes were upon some vision in which he could not share and had no part.

Even as I watched, the woman rose to depart, and I saw that she was swathed in a loose, burnous-like garment that had no relation to fashion, and upon her feet were sandals. The man also rose, but she checked him with a gesture, and her voice came to us across the room.

"You promised you would not try to follow me, Pat," she said.

The man who was between her and the door paused irresolutely, and then he flashed out with pent-up vehemence: "He's ruining you," he cried. "Body and soul, he's ruining you. Let me get at him and I'll break his neck if I hang for it."

"It is useless," was the reply. "You can do nothing. Let me pass. Nothing you can do will make any difference."

The man lifted both arms above his head, and though his back was to us, we could see his whole body shaking with passion.

"Curse him!" he cried. "Curse him! May the Black Curse of Michael be upon him!"

The Irish brogue, unleashed by emotion, rolled from his lips, and seemed to add pungency to his curses, if that were possible. The startled waitresses, in their gaudy cretonne overalls, huddled in a corner, staring, and an obese manageress waddled from some sanctum behind a bead curtain, but before she could intervene, the woman in the burnous, with a quick lithe movement, had slipped round the little table and out of the door into the dusk, and the man turning hastily to follow her, fell right over Taverner's legs and came all asprawl on to our tea table.

He dropped into the nearest chair, white and shaken from his passion, while we gazed ruefully at smashed crockery and streaming milk.

He was the first to recover himself, and passing his hand

194

across his forehead in a dazed way, seemed to awaken from his nightmare.

"I beg your pardon," he said, the Irish brogue vanished from his speech. "A thousand apologies. Here, waitress, clear up these gentlemen's table and bring them another tea."

The manageress waddled up, glaring at him, and he turned to her.

"I cannot apologize sufficiently," he said. "I was greatly upset by—by domestic trouble, and I fear my feelings got the better of me."

He lay back in his chair as if completely exhausted. "It's lost she is, body and soul," he muttered, more to himself than to us. " 'Pray to the Blessed Virgin,' said Father O'Hara, and so I have—for her, but it's to the Holy Michael I'll pray for Josephus, may the Black Curse be upon him!"

Taverner leaned forward and laid his hand gently on the man's arm.

"It seems as if your prayers have been heard," he said, "for not half an hour ago we saw Josephus taken off to hospital with a nasty scalp wound. I don't know what your complaint against him may be," he continued, "but I know Josephus, and I should imagine it is amply justified."

"You know Josephus?" said the man, staring at us dazedly.

"I do," said Taverner, "and I may as well tell you that I am 'after' him myself on one or two little accounts, and I think I have the means of bringing him to book, so may I suggest that we make common cause against him?" And he laid his card on the little table before the shaken, grey-faced man in front of us.

"Taverner, Dr. Taverner," said the stranger thoughtfully as he fingered the card. "I have heard that name somewhere. Did you not once meet a man called Coates in a curious affair over a stolen manuscript?"

"I did," said Taverner.

"They always said there was more in that matter than met the eye," said our new acquaintance. "But I never believed in such things till I saw what Josephus could do."

He looked at Taverner keenly out of deep-set eyes.

"I believe you are the one man in London who would be of any use in the matter," he said.

"If I can, I shall be glad to assist you," replied Taverner, "for, as I said before, I know Josephus."

"My name's McDermot," said our new acquaintance, "and that lady you saw with me was my wife. I say 'was my wife,' " he added, the flame of passion lighting up again in his dark eyes, "for she is gone from me now. Josephus has taken her. No, not in the ordinary sense," he added hastily lest our thought should smirch her, "but into that extraordinary group of his that he does his seances with, and she is as much lost to me as if she had entered a nunnery. Do you wonder that I curse the man who has broken up my home? If he had taken her because he loved her I could have pardoned him more easily, but there is no question of love in this; he has taken her because he wants to use her for some purpose of his own, just as he has taken lots of other women, and whatever it is she will lose her soul. This thing is evil, I tell you," he continued, with renewed excitement. "I don't know what it is, but I know it's evil. You have only to look at the man to see that he is evil right through, and she thinks he's a saint, an inspired teacher, an adept, whatever you call it," he added bitterly. "But I tell you, men don't grow faces like that on clean living and high thinking."

"Can you give me any information as to his doings? I have lost touch with Josephus since the last time he had to leave the country, but I imagine he is doing much the same sort of thing he used to do."

"So far as I know," said McDermot, "he appeared on the scene about a year ago from no one knows where, and advertised classes in psychic development. That brought him in touch with various people who are interested in that sort of thing—I'm not, my Church doesn't allow it, and I don't wonder—Mary, that's my wife, used to belong to a sort of occult club that Coates ran in St. John's Wood; Coates being a fool, took up Josephus, burnt his fingers with him, and dropped him, but not before he had got hold of two or three women out of that set, my wife among them. Then Josephus seemed to find his feet and thrive amazingly. (He had been a pretty seedy-looking adventurer when he first turned up.) And now he has got a house somewhere, though nobody except those who are in the secret knows where, and he has got, so my wife says, a group of women who help him in his work. Exactly what it is that they do, I don't know, but he seems to have got a tremendous hold on them. They all seem to be in love with him, and yet they live peaceably in the same house. It is an amazing affair altogether. It is not money he is after in his inner circle though he gets plenty of that from the rest of his devotees, but, so far as I can make out, a particular type of physique, and it appears to me that, as he thrives, they go down hill. At any rate, he has to introduce fresh blood into his group periodically, and sometimes there is a desperate hunt for a new recruit while Josephus slowly wilts, and then, having got a fresh favourite, he seems suddenly to take on a new lease of life. The whole thing is queer, and uncanny, and unsavoury, and even before it broke up my home I couldn't bear it."

Taverner nodded. "He has done much the same sort of thing several times already. It may interest you to know that I assisted in thrashing Josephus and ducking him in a horse trough in my student days after we had had a succession of his victims in our wards. There was a society working on his system then; but I believe it was stamped out as an organisation. However, he seems to be restarting it, so the sooner we take him in hand the better, lest he get a foothold in the subconscious mind of the nation. Such a thing is possible you know."

"You can count on me," said McDermot, holding out a

sinewy hand, his eyes sparkling with the light of battle. "The first thing we have to do is to find out where his house is, and the next to get into it, and then—'Once aboard the lugger and the maid is mine,' as the song says."

"With regard to the first, that is already accomplished," said Taverner. "The second is the problem that immediately confronts us, but I believe it to be capable of solution; but as to the third, I am not so sure; Josephus will hold those women in the unseen world in a way which you do not understand, and it will be very difficult to free them without their cooperation, and almost impossible to obtain their cooperation. I have often dealt with these cases before, and know their difficulties. An infatuated woman at any time is difficult to deal with, but when they have been initiated into a fraternity with ritual they are almost impossible. The first thing to do, however, is to gain a foothold in that house by some means or other."

"I think I can help you there," I said, "I can call and offer to give evidence as to the accident, and then worm myself in as a convert."

"That is an idea with possibilities," said Taverner, "though I am not sure that Josephus will look upon additional Adams as an asset to his Eden, but a doctor always has his value, especially when you are doing risky things you want kept quiet. There is a whole nest of hospitals round here that he might have been taken to; phone them up till you find out where he went, represent yourself as a member of the family to the hospitals, and a member of the hospital to the family, and chance your luck. This is a hunt after my own heart. A slimier villain never wanted exterminating, and Josephus is no light-weight. He will put up a fight worth seeing."

The early diners were arriving at the little tea-room, and our party broke up with mutual expressions of good will, Taverner to return to Hindhead, and McDermot and I to the telephone. My first guess proved to be the right one. Josephus had been taken to the Middlesex, had his head

198

sewn up, and been sent home. So, sending McDermot off to wait for me in the oyster dive in Tottenham Court Road, I went round to a square not fifty yards away, and there rang the bell of an imposing looking house whose lower windows were shuttered in an inhospitable fashion.

The door was opened by a girl in a loose blue burnous, and to her I stated my business. She seemed quite unsuspicious and conducted me into an ordinary enough dining-room where in a few minutes an older woman came to me. She was a tall woman, and at some time must have been handsome, but her face was drawn, haggard and strained, to the last degree, and I thought of McDermot's remark that Josephus' pupils wilted as their master throve.

I could see that she was on her guard, though anxious for my assistance, but my tale was a perfectly straight-forward one and had the additional advantage of being true so far as it went. I was standing on the island when Josephus was knocked down. I rendered first aid, but did not stop to give my name and address to the policeman because I was in a hurry, but took this, the first opportunity of repairing the omission. There was no flaw in my statement, and she accepted it, but when I backed it with my card bearing the Harley Street address I saw her suddenly become abstracted.

"Excuse me a moment," she said, and hastily left the room.

She was gone more than a moment, and I began to wonder whether my scheme had miscarried and what my chances were of getting out of the house without unpleasantness, when she reappeared.

"I should be so grateful," she said, "if you would come to Dr. Josephus' room and have a little talk with him."

"So far as I am concerned, I should be quite willing, but a head injury ought to be kept quiet," I said, my medical self triumphing over me in my new role of conspirator. To my relief she brushed aside my objection.

"It will do more good than harm," she said, "because

199

if he takes to you, we may be able to get him to let you attend him. He is a very tiresome person to deal with." She added with a smile, as of a mother speaking of her spoilt darling of whom even the naughtinesses are adorable.

She led me, not upstairs, but down into the basement, and there, in what had probably been a scullery looking out into a back yard, we found Josephus. The room was as amazing as the man. Walls, floor, and ceiling were jet black, so that the room was a hollow cube of gleaming darkness lit only by a shaded lamp that stood at Josephus' elbow. He himself was not in bed, as I had expected, but lay upon the piled up cushions of a divan, robed in the burnous which seemed to be the universal wear of this strange fraternity. In his case it was a flaming scarlet, and lying back among his cushions, with his strange sallow face surmounted by white bandages, he looked as if he had stepped straight out of the Arabian Nights.

The tall woman subsided among her draperies on a stool at Josephus' side, and he, with a wave of his hand, invited me to be seated on the edge of the divan. He looked amazingly fit in spite of the fact that he had had his head laid open at five o'clock that afternoon, and even I, man though I am and knowing what I did of his record, could feel the extraordinary fascination of his personality.

The tall woman made us known to each other, and one could almost see her anxiously smoothing his feathers and turning her pet about to make him exhibit himself at his best angle, and he, nothing loth, set himself out to make a favourable impression. I could imagine invisible fingers feeling all over my soul to find out the best way of handling me. I felt that his willingness to consult me was a quick opportunism; it was I who was to be in his hands, not he in mine, and I remembered Taverner's words that a doctor was a useful thing when risky work that needed concealment was afoot.

We talked for a few minutes, but I felt that he had no

intention of pressing the case against the chauffeur, probably valuing his privacy more highly than any compensation he was likely to get; all the same, he pretended to want my evidence, but I put my foot down.

"Look here, sir," I said. "You have had a certain amount of concussion, and the one thing for you is darkness and quiet. I will come to see you again in a few days when you are in a condition to go into the matter, which you are not now. But at the present moment not another word will I say unless I can be of any use to you in my professional capacity."

I saw by the tall woman's amazed expression that Josephus was not accustomed to be talked to in this fashion, but he took it quite amicably.

"Ah," he said, with a grin which roused all my latent animosity against the man, "I have resources that you ordinary medical men know nothing of." And we parted with mutual expressions of esteem.

I picked up McDermot at the oyster dive, and he took me back to the flat that had been his home, where it was arranged that I was to stop for the next few days pending developments with Josephus. The rooms bore pathetic witness to the truth of his story. I could see the disordered evidences which told me that he had first put away all the things that could remind him of his wife, and then, in desperation, got them out again. We settled down with our pipes amid the neglect and muddle, and McDermot went over the story for the twentieth time. He could tell me nothing I did not already know by heart, but the telling of it seemed to relieve him. It was the old story of the paddler who got into deep water, striking those unsuspected potholes in the unseen which for ever threaten bathers who cannot swim if they venture into those dark and uncharted waters.

I did not call on Josephus next day, for I did not want to appear too pressing, but the following day I rang him up on the phone. The great man himself answered my call

201

and was more than cordial.

"I wish I had known where to find you," he said. "I should have asked you to come round yesterday."

I picked up a taxi, and was soon at the house whose lower shutters seemed to be kept permanently closed. Once again I was taken to the strange subterranean sanctum which seemed so appropriate a setting for that rococo personality which was known to us as Dr. Josephus. His head was naturally still in bandages, though the burnous had given place to a grey lounge suit, but even so, he would have been a marked man anywhere. I had thought Taverner the strangest personality I had ever met, but he was normal compared to Josephus.

He made coffee himself in the Turkish fashion, produced cigarettes rolled in a curious golden paper of a type I had never met before, and set himself to the task of intriguing my imagination, in which, in spite of my knowledge of his record, he certainly succeeded. Like Taverner, his culture was encyclopaedic, and he seemed to have traveled off the beaten track in most parts of the world. I admit quite frankly that I thoroughly enjoyed myself. It did not take long before the talk edged round to occultism, in which I avowed my interest, and then Josephus began to spread his feathers, cautiously at first, as if to see if the ice would bear, and then he opened his heart when he found that I had some knowledge of the subject and did not appear to be over-burdened with moral scruples.

"The trouble with this sort of thing," I said, "is that although one can hear any amount about the theory, it is extraordinarily difficult to get hold of anything tangible. Either the people who do all the writing and lecturing haven't got any real knowledge, or else they haven't got the nerve to put it into practice."

He rose to my bait like a fish. "Ah," he said, "you have hit the right nail on the head. Precious few men have the nerve for practical occultism," and he preened himself in a way that told me where the man's weak spot lay.

Josephus paused for a moment and seemed to weigh me in the balance, and then, watching me carefully and choosing every word, he began to speak.

"I suppose you know," he said, "that a very little development would render you psychic?"

I was frankly surprised, and, I admit it, secretly flattered, for I had always been held up as the archetype of materialistic stolidity. Then I remembered that Taverner had often laughingly quoted these very words as the stock opening of charlatanism, and I pulled myself together, with a sudden angry defensiveness, for it startled me to see the extent to which Josephus had obtained empire over my imagination during our short intercourse. I hid my uneasiness, however, and returned his lead in kind.

"Psychism is all right so far as it goes," I said, "but what I am really interested in is ritual magic."

It was a bow drawn at a venture, and I saw that I had overshot the mark, as I generally do when I try to swim with the brass pots in the deep waters of occultism. Josephus did not quite like it; why, I could not make out, and he seemed to edge away from me mentally.

"Know much about ritual magic?" he asked with an assumption of ease which I felt sure he did not feel.

I did not know what he was driving at, and not wishing to be caught out, I followed Mark Twain's advice, and fell back upon the truth.

"No," I said frankly, "I do not." And, catching the look of relief on Josephus' face, I added mentally to myself, "And neither do you."

He spoke again, pausing impressively between each word.

"If you are in earnest, and are prepared to take the risk, I can show you something that very few men alive at the present time have even dreamt of. But," he continued, and I saw that his quick brain was rapidly maturing a scheme, "I shall have to test you first."

I bid him name his test.

Still eyeing me closely, evidently trying each step and ready to back away from his intention the instant I showed any sign of uneasiness, he continued:

"I shall test first," he said, "your incipient psychism, by seeing whether you have sufficient intuition to discern my intentions towards you and trust me without question."

I thought that this was the neatest presentation of the confidence trick I had ever met, and bowed my assent.

"You will come tonight at a quarter to nine to the alley that runs at the back of these houses; the coal cellar opens on to it, and I will be there to admit you. You must wait in the coal cellar until I have re-entered the house, and you hear sounds of chanting, and then you must come through the other door of the coal cellar, which communicates with the yard. The bars of that window take out if you push them downwards, and they are held in place by springs, and you can get into this room, but be sure to replace the bars, I don't want anyone to find 'em loose. In here you will find behind the cushions a bright scarlet robe with a cowl like an Inquisitor's. Put it on and pull the cowl right down over your face, there are eye-holes in it, and walk boldly upstairs to the first floor and give five knocks on the drawing-room door. When the door is opened, say 'In the name of the Council of Seven, Peace be unto you,' and walk right in and up to me; I shall be cowled the same as you, but you will know me because my robe is also scarlet. I shall be on a dias at the end of the room. When you get up to me, I shall rise, and we will shake hands, and then you will take my chair, and I shall sit at your right. You will stretch out your hand and say:

" 'I come in the name of the Great Chiefs.' "

"Then we will proceed to business. You will answer yes or no, to any question you are asked, but nothing more. And if you fail—" and he pushed his ugly face right into mine, "you will have to reckon with the Unseen Forces which you have invoked. Is that clear?"

"Perfectly clear," I said. "Only I am not sure that I can

204

remember it all, and how am I to know whether to answer yes or no?"

"You will watch me out of the corner of your eye. If I stir my right foot, you will answer yes, if I stir my left, you will answer no. I shan't move 'em much, so you must keep a sharp look-out. And when I fold my hands you must stand up, say 'It is finished,' and walk out. Come down here and clear out the way you came, being careful to see that the red robe is well hidden under the cushions, the bars replaced, and the coal cellar door shut."

When Josephus finished he looked me straight in the eyes with a very steady gaze, which I returned equally steadily. I allowed a moment to elapse before I replied, for I did not want to appear to accept with too great alacrity.

"I'll take it on," I said.

A gleam of satisfaction lit up Josephus' curious eyes; he looked very much like a jackdaw who has secreted some bauble.

We parted the best of friends, and I returned to Harley Street, where Taverner, having finished the day's interviews, was awaiting me.

I recounted the conversation that had taken place, and Taverner was immensely intrigued.

"That tells me a great many things," he said. "I agree with you that Josephus is not a trained occultist, but he knows a great deal about the secret side of both sex and drugs, and he is a very clever manipulator of human nature and loves intrigue for its own sake, as this scheme of his shows."

"What do you make of it?" I said. "What is he driving at?"

"I should say that his group was getting restless," said Taverner. "He evidently does not take them into his confidence, *vide* the window bars. You are apparently designed to appear as some messenger of higher powers whom he has invoked in support of his authority. This leads me to believe that he is conducting a one man show, and this taken in conjunction with what we suppose to be his ignorance of ritual magic, makes me think that he never has been initiated into any fraternity. But, my God, if he had been, what wouldn't he have done if he had had a knowledge of the Names of Power in addition to his natural gifts! The fraternities are well guarded, Rhodes, we don't often have a traitor.

"Now come along, we have just got nice time for a meal before the evening's entertainment."

We went to the restaurant in Soho where the metaphysical head waiter, who appeared to be interested in the same subjects as Taverner, held sway. Of course we had our usual warm but respectful welcome and were led to a retired table, and as the metaphysician hovered round us with the wine list, Taverner beckoned him nearer and said:

"Giuseppi, we are going this evening to number seven, Malvern Square, near Gower Street. It has a back entrance into the alley behind, and the bars of a window looking into the back yard can be removed by pressing them down. Ring me up at Harley Street at ten o'clock to-morrow morning, and if I am not back, take steps in the matter. You know what to do."

As soon as we were alone Taverner produced a small silver pocket flash and a pad of gauze, which he passed to me under cover of the table cloth.

"That's chloroform," he said. "Have the pad ready and clap it over his nose as soon as he opens the door. I have got a length of cord in my pocket. Josephus is not going to appear in this act."

"But what am I going to do when I am sitting in the seats of the mighty and Josephus isn't there to twiddly his toes when they ask awkward questions?" I said anxiously.

"Wait and see," said Taverner. I noticed that beside his chair was a small suit case.

We timed our arrival in the back alley just nicely, and I heard a crunching of the coals that betokened Josephus' advent, just as I was putting the chloroform on to the pad.

"No!" whispered Taverner, and I knocked softly on the grimy door.

It opened an inch.

"That you, Rhodes?" whispered a voice from the darkness. "Come in quietly, they're all about, damn them. Fussing with the supper things. Why can't women leave things alone?" The voice sounded bad-tempered.

"Where are you, old chap?" I said, feeling for him in the darkness. My hand touched his throat and instantly closed on it. I clapped the pad over his face and thrust him backward with my whole strength. Down he went on to the coals with me on top of him. He was a powerful man and struggled like a cat, but I was much the bigger, and he hadn't a chance. His struggles slackened as the chloroform got in its work, and when Taverner, who had been securing the door, flashed a hooded torch upon us, I was kneeling on his inanimate form.

Taverner tied him up with an expertness which indicated experience, and then cast about for somewhere to conceal him.

"I don't want him discovered prematurely, if anyone should want a scuttle of coals," he said.

"Why not dig a hole and bury him?" I suggested, having thoroughly entered into the spirit of the place. "Here's a shovel. Make a hole and stick him in up to the neck, and put that old bottomless bucket over his head."

Taverner chuckled, and in two minutes Josephus was as if he had never been, and leaving him thus very indecently interred, we made our way cautiously into the yard. It was pitch black, but my knowledge of the geography of the place enabled me to find the window, and in less time than it takes to tell, we had dislodged the bars, got in, switched on the light, and locked the door on the inside.

"Here's your garment," said Taverner, pulling a flowing scarlet robe from under the sofa cushions and inducting me into it with a knowledge of its anatomy which pointed to previous experience.

207

There was a soft knock at the door and I held my breath. "Are you ready, dearest? They are all assembled," said a feminine voice.

"Go on in and begin," snarled Taverner, in a voice so exactly like Josephus' that I involuntarily looked over my shoulder.

We heard the footsteps die away down the passage, (evidently Josephus had taught them not to argue), and in a few minutes the sound of chanting broke out overhead.

Taverner opened his suitcase and took out the most wonderful robes I have ever seen in my life. Stiff with embroidery and heavy with bullion, the great cope looked like the mines of Ophir in the shaded light of that sombre room. Taverner put it on over an emerald green soutane and I fastened the jewelled clasp upon his breast. Then he handed to me, for he could not raise his arms, the Headdress of Egypt, and I placed it on his head. I have never seen such a sight. The gaunt lineaments of Taverner framed in the Egyptian drapery, his tall figure made gigantic by the cope, and the jewelled ankh in his hand (which I was thankful to see was sufficiently heavy to be effective as a weapon)—made a picture which I shall remember to my dying day. Every time he moved, the incense of many rituals floated from the folds of his garments, the silk rustled, the gold-work clinked; it seemed as if a priest-king of lost Atlantis had come, in response to an invocation, to claim the obedience of his worshippers.

We went up the narrow stairs into the darkened hall, and thence to the drawing-room floor, where a smell of incense told us that we were upon the right track. Taverner smote upon the door five times, and we heard a voice say: "Guardian of the Gate, see who seeks admission."

The door opened, and we were confronted by a plump and dumpy figure robed and cowled in black, which nearly went over backwards at sight of Taverner. My scarlet robe evidently led the doorkeeper to mistake me for Josephus, for we were admitted without demur, and found

208

ourselves in what was evidently the temple of the strange worship which he conducted.

I made straight for the dais, as I had been instructed, and sat down before they could notice my height, and I am pretty certain that they all thought their usual magus was in the chair. Taverner, however, advanced to the altar, and extending the golden ankh towards the assembly, said in that resonant voice of his:

"Peace to all beings."

This was evidently the opening they expected, for the figure on a raised dais at the far end of the room, which from its height I judged to be the tall woman, replied:

"From whom do you bring greeting?"

"I do not bring it," said Taverner. "I give it."

This was evidently not the right cue, and threw the whole lodge into confusion, but so completely did Taverner dominate them, that it was they, not he, who did not know their part.

All eyes turned to me, believing me to be Josephus, but I sat like a graven image and gave no sign.

Then Taverner spoke again.

"The name of the Council of Seven has been invoked, and I who am the Senior of Seven, have come unto you. Know me by this sign," and he extended his hand. On the fore-finger flashed a great ring. I don't believe any one in the room was any the wiser, but the lodge officers, who were supposed to know, were ashamed to admit they didn't, and the rank and file naturally followed their lead.

There was dead silence in the room, which was suddenly broken by a rustle of drapery as a figure upon a third dais on my left arose, and I heard the voice of Mary McDermot speaking.

"I ask pardon for my lack of faith," she said. "It was I who invoked the Council of Seven because I believed them to be non-existent. But I realize my error. I see the power and I acknowledge it. Your face tells me of your greatness, the vibrations of your personality tell me of your truth and goodness. I recognize and I obey."

Taverner turned towards her.

"How came it that you believed the Council of Seven to be non-existent?" He demanded in that great resonant voice of his.

"Because my husband's importunities had come between me and my duty to the Order. Because his prayers and invocations of the saints had spread like a cloud between me and the brightness of the Master's face, so that I could not see his glory, and believed him to be a vulgar sensualist and charlatan, taking advantage of our credulity."

"My daughter," said Taverner, and his voice was very gentle, "do you believe in me?"

"I do," she cried. "I not only believe, I know. It is you I have seen in my dreams, you are the initiator I have always sought. The Master Josephus promised he would bring me to you, and he has kept his word."

"Approach the altar," commanded Taverner.

She came and knelt before him unbidden. He touched her forehead with the golden ankh, and I saw her sway at the touch.

"From the Unreal, lead me to the Real. From Darkness bring me to Light. From Impurity cleanse me and sanctify me," came the deep resonant voice. Then he took her by the hand and raised her, and placed her beside me on the dais.

Taverner returned to the altar and took his stand before it and surveyed the room. Then from under his cope he produced a curiously wrought metal box. He opened one end and took out of it a handful of white powder and strewed it upon the altar in the form of a cross.

"Unclean," he said, and his voice was like the tolling of a bell.

He opened the other end of the box and took out a handful of ashes, and these also he strewed upon the altar, defiling its white linen covering.

"Unclean," he said again.

210

He stretched forth his ankh, and with the head of it extinguished the lamp that burnt upon the altar.

"Unclean," he said a third time, and as he did so, all sense of power seemed to leave the room, and it became flat, ordinary, and rather tawdry. Taverner alone seemed real, all the rest were make-believe. He seemed like a live man in a room full of waxworks.

He turned, and I rose, and with the girl between us, we left the room in the midst of dead silence. I closed the door softly behind us, and, finding that the key was in the lock, took the precaution to turn it.

In the darkened hall, unlit save for the rays of a street lamp through the fanlight, Taverner confronted the bewildered girl. She had pushed back her cowl, and her bright hair fell in disorder about her face. He placed his hands on her shoulder.

"My daughter," he said. "You cannot advance save by the path of duty. You cannot rise to the higher life on broken faith and neglected obligations. The man who has given his name and heart into your keeping cannot have a home unless you make him one; cannot have a child unless you give him one. You may free yourself from him, but he cannot free himself from you. In this incarnation you have elected to choose the Path of the Hearth-fire, and therefore no other is open to you. Return, and see that the fire is lit and that hearth swept and garnished, and I will come to you and show you how illumination may be obtained upon that Path. You have invoked the Council of Seven, and have therefore come under the discipline of the Council of Seven, and coming under the discipline, you have come under the protection. Depart in peace."

And he opened the door and put her outside.

We hastily collected our impedimenta and followed her. A violent ringing of electric bells in the basement showed that the people upstairs had discovered that they were locked in.

The night drive down to Hindhead cleared my brain,

which whirled strangely. A vision of Taverner in cope and head-dress danced before my eyes, which the everyday appearance of my chief in frieze overcoat and muffler did nothing to allay. At length we reached our destination, put the car to bed, and stood for a moment under the tranquil stars before entering the silent house, long since wrapt in slumber, and as I thought of the events of the evening I seemed to move in a dream. Suddenly recollection hit me on the solar plexus and I woke with a start.

"Taverner!" I said, "supposing someone delivers a load of coals on top of Josephus—?"

A Son of the Night

It was not often that people attempted to 'use' Taverner for their own ends, and it was only because the Countess of Cullan was so sure of her powers that the attempt was made. She was a very great lady, though somewhat blown upon as to reputation; she had reason to believe in her power over men, and never doubted that Taverner and I, given sufficient encouragement, would worship at her well-served shrine. She was a neighbour of ours, the grounds of the nursing home, in fact, being carved out of the Cullan estate during the days when the old earl was using capital as income. The present earl was a man of a very different type; so different, in fact, from what might have been expected of a scion of the house of Cullan, that rumour had it that he was 'not quite all there.' Be that as it may, he was at least 'there' enough to keep a tight hand on the family finances and insisted on allowing the goose of capital to lay the golden eggs of interest instead of having it killed then and there to assuage the family hunger. This, rumour added, was a very sore point, and productive of much rancour in the home life.

The opening move in the game took place when Taverner and I were invited to a garden party at Cullan Court, and needless to say, did not go. The next move was when the Countess drove over in her two-seater and insisted that I should return forthwith to make up a set at tennis. I was cornered and could not escape; and, having been assigned my flapper, duly patted balls over the net at the Honourable John, younger brother of the earl, and his flapper, who returned them in a resigned kind of fashion, till we came to the conclusion that a single might not, after all, be without its charms, deposited our flappers in the shade, and set to work in earnest.

Having a long reach, a steady eye, and a good wind, I take kindly to games, though they are not my enthusiasm as they are with some people who are able to acquit themselves adequately; to the Honourable John, however, sport took the place of religion, and in whatever game he played he had to excel; and to give him his due, he generally succeeded in doing so.

In the first set he beat me after a struggle; in the second set I beat him in a thrilling contest, and in the third we settled down to a life-and-death battle. All his debonair charm was gone, and the face that looked at me across the net was positively malignant as the score slowly turned against him. When the game concluded in my favour, it was all he could do to remember his manners. The cloud soon blew away, however, and after a pleasant tea on the terrace, the Countess drove me home again with her own fair hands. I had grown much more inclined to accept future invitations.

But, although I was quite willing to play the Honourable John at tennis, I was distinctly anxious to steer clear of the Countess, for, though old enough to be my aunt, if not my mother, she blatantly flirted with me.

A dinner party was arranged shortly after that; Taverner could not escape it, even with all his wiliness, and duly led in the Countess, who, to my intense amusement, flirted with him also. I had the very pretty daughter (who seemed to take after her mother in more than her looks) for my partner. But while the mother appeared bent on making an impression on Taverner, the daughter seemed equally bent on making me realise that I had made an impression on her, and each glanced at the other occasionally to see how she was getting on. It gave me an odd and unpleasant feeling to see these two women of a great family making a 'dead set' at a couple of commoners like Taverner and my-

214

self; and as I saw Taverner succumbing to the lure I got more and more disgusted, sulky, and silent with my companion until it struck me that there might be a method in Taverner's madness; he was, at the best of times, the least impressionable of men, and very unlikely to be attracted by this overblown rose of a woman who was wooing him so blatantly. So I in my turn allowed myself to succumb to the daughter, and received in exchange the confidence that there was a great sorrow in their lives, and that she herself was under the shadow of fear and felt dire need of the protection of a masculine arm. Did I ever ride out on the moors? She did, every morning, so perhaps some day we might meet, far from watching eyes, and then, perhaps, I might be able to help her with a little advice, for she felt the need of a man's advice. For nothing more than advice did she ask upon this occasion, and then she changed the subject.

They disgusted me, these women. They were so blatant and sure of their power to charm. It also struck me as strange that the master of the house not only never appeared, but was never referred to; he might have been non-existent for all the part he played in this elaborate menage, which seemed to be run by the mother for the exclusive benefit of herself and her two younger children.

"Taverner," I said as we drove away, "what do you suppose they want with us?"

"They have not shown their hand yet," he answered, "but I do not fancy we shall be kept long in suspense. They are not exactly backward in coming forward."

As we came out of the park gates, Taverner suddenly swerved the car just in time to avoid someone who was entering, and I saw for a moment in the glare of the headlights a strange-looking face—high-cheekboned, hook-nosed, and haggard, with a rough crop of unkempt black hair surmounting it. The darkness swallowed him up and he vanished without a word spoken, yet he left upon me the impression that I had seen someone who mattered. I

215

cannot express it more clearly than that nor give a reason for my feeling, yet he impressed me as being far more than a random pedestrian whom we had nearly run down. His face haunted me, I could not get it out of my mind; I had a curious feeling that I had seen it somewhere before—and then it suddenly came to me where I had seen it. In a neighboring village lived an old parson who had a very similar cast of countenance; probably the stranger was a son, or even a grandson of his; but what was he doing, going hatless up to Cullan Court at that hour of the night, I could not imagine.

I did not ride with that scion of nobility, the Lady Mary, but Taverner hobnobbed shamelessly with her formidable parent.

"I have had my instructions," he said, and no other explanation would he give; but for me nowadays no other explanation was needed, for I knew quite well that there were Those under which Taverner worked, just as I worked under him, though They were not of this plane of existence. I do not think that at the time Taverner himself had any inkling of what was afoot; he merely knew that here was a matter in which Those to whom he looked desired him to take a hand, and so he gave the Countess of Cullan opportunity to develop her intrigues in her own way, biding his time.

The intrigue took longer than we expected to develop, and I began to suspect that the Countess was as anxious for its conclusion as we were. At last the opportunity for which she had been waiting arrived, and she phoned for us to come at once. Her eldest son, it seems, was having one of his attacks, and she wanted Taverner to see him actually in the throes of it, and was therefore anxious for his speedy arrival lest the invalid should recover and cease to be interesting. She expressly desired that I should come too; the reason for this she would explain upon our arrival as she did not care to confide it over the telephone.

Ten minutes in the car brought us to Cullan Court, and

we were shown forthwith into the boudoir of the Countess, a room as pink and overblown as she. In a few seconds she came in, clad in filmy black, followed by her daughter in virginal white; they made a lovely picture for those who like stage effects, but I am afraid I despised the two women too heartily to appreciate them. A minute later the Honourable John came in also, and supported by her family, the Countess opened her heart to us.

"We have a great sorrow in our lives, Dr. Taverner, upon which we want to ask your advice and help—and yours, too, Dr. Rhodes," she added, including me as an afterthought.

I was of the opinion that exasperation rather than sorrow would best describe their condition, but I bowed politely and said nothing.

"You are so sympathetic," she continued to my partner, my existence having once more slipped her memory. "You have such wonderful insight. I knew as soon as I met you that you would understand, and I was sure also" here she lowered her voice to a whisper—"that you would help." She laid her hand upon Taverner's sleeve and gazed back. The Honourable John turned his back and looked out of the window, and I felt pretty certain that he shared with me an irresistible desire to burst out laughing.

"It is my eldest son, poor Marius," continued the Countess. "I am afraid we have got to face the fact that he is quite, quite insane." She paused, and dabbed her eyes. "We have delayed and delayed as long as ever we could, perhaps too long. Perhaps, if we had had him treated earlier we might have saved him. Don't you think so, John?"

"No, I don't," said John. "He has been mad as a March hare ever since I can remember, and ought to have been locked up before he got big enough to be dangerous."

"Yes, I am afraid we have not acted rightly by him," said the Countess, taking refuge in her handkerchief again. "We should have had him certified long ago."

217

"Certification is not a form of treatment," said Taverner drily.

The Honourable John darted a somewhat unpleasant look at my colleague, opened his mouth as if to speak, thought better of it, and shut it again.

"The time has come," said the Countess, "when we have got to face it. I must part with my poor darling for the sake of my other children."

We bowed sympathetically.

"Would you like to see him?" she asked.

We bowed again.

Up the heavily carpeted stairs we went, and along a far wing to a bedroom which I should imagine the owner had occupied as a boy. We crossed the worn oilcloth on the floor, and saw before us, lying insensible upon a narrow iron bedstead, the man whom we had nearly run over at the park gates, and whom I had set down as the son or grandson of the old cleric in the neighbouring village.

Taverner stood gazing down upon the unconscious form for some time without speaking, while the Countess and her son watched him closely and with increasing uneasiness as the moments lengthened out.

At last he said, "I cannot certify a man because I find him unconscious."

"We can tell you all his symptoms, if that is what you want," said the Honourable John.

"Neither would that be enough," said Taverner, "I must see for myself."

"Then you doubt our word?" said John, looking ugly.

"Not at all," said Taverner, "but I must fulfill the requirements of the law and certify from observation, not hearsay."

He turned suddenly to the Countess. "Who is your usual medical man?" he demanded.

She hesitated a moment. "Dr. Parkes," she said reluctantly.

"What does he say about the case?"

"We are not satisfied with his treatment. We—we don't think he is sufficiently careful."

I thought to myself that Dr. Parkes had probably also been asked to certify, and had also declined.

"If you want to see," said the Honourable John, "we can soon show you," and he dipped the fringe of a towel in the water-jug, tore open the pajama jacket, and began to flick the chest of the unconscious man. His action revealed a body wasted to skeleton thinness on which angry red weals sprange up at each blow of the knotted threads. The end of a fringed towel, weighted with water, is a cruel weapon, as I well knew from my school days, and it was all I could do to keep myself from interfering; but Taverner remained immobile, watching, and I let myself be guided by his example.

This drastic method of resuscitation soon produced twitchings of the unconscious form, and then spasmodic movements of the limbs, which finally coordinated themselves into definite attempts at self-defense. It was like the struggles of a sleeper fighting in nightmare, and when the eyes at last opened, they had the dazed, bewildered look of a man suddenly roused from deep sleep in strange surroundings. He plainly did not know where he was; neither did he recognise the people standing around him, and he was evidently prepared to resist to the limits of his strength all efforts to control him. Those limits were soon reached, however, and he lay immobile in the powerful hands of his brother, watching us with strange, filmy eyes and uttering neither word nor sound.

"You see for yourself," said John triumphantly. Lady Cullan dabbed her eyes with a wisp of a lace handkerchief.

"I am afraid it is hopeless," she said. "We cannot keep him at home any longer. Where would you advise us to send him, Doctor Taverner?"

"I would be prepared to take charge of him," said Taverner, "if you would be willing to entrust him to me."

The Countess clasped her hands. "Oh, what a relief!"

she cried. "What a blessed relief from the anxiety that has burdened us for so many years!"

"You will get the formalities through as soon as possible, won't you Doctor?" said the Honourable John. "There are a lot of business matters that want attending to, and we shall need your certificate in order to take them over."

Taverner dry-washed his hands and bowed unctuously.

II

I, meanwhile, had been watching the man on the bed, whom every one else seemed to have forgotten. I could see that he was gathering together his scattered wits and was attuned to the position in which he found himself. He looked at Taverner and myself as if taking our measure, and then lay still, listening to the conversation.

I bent over him.

"My name is Rhodes," I said, "Dr. Rhodes, and that is Dr. Taverner. Lady Cullan was alarmed at your illness and sent over to the nursing home for us."

He looked me straight in the face, and his eyes had a keenness that seemed to go right through me.

"It appears to me," he said, "that you are engaged in certifying me as insane."

I shrugged my shoulders. "I should need to know a great deal more about a case than I know about you," I replied, "before I should be willing to put my name to a certificate."

"But do you not deny that you have been called in for the purpose of certifying me?"

"No," I said, "I don't see why I should deny it, for it is a fact that we have."

"Good God," he exclaimed, "have I not got the right to live my own life in my own way without being certified insane and having my liberty taken from me? What harm have I ever done to anyone? Who has any complaint

220

against me except my brother? And why should I sell my land to pay his debts and turn better men than he out of their holdings? I tell you, I will not sell the land. To me, land is sacred."

He stopped abruptly, as if afraid that he had said too much, and eyed me uneasily to see how I had taken this last statement. Then he continued.

"If I am deprived of my liberty I shall not live. I do not want the money. What I have, I give them already, but I will not part with the land. I draw my life from it. Take the land from me, take me from the land, and I tell you that it will not live—and neither shall I!"

He raised his voice in his excitement, and attracted the attention of the group at the other side of the room. The face of the Honourable John was wreathed in a smile of triumphant satisfaction at this outburst, and the Countess had again occasion to apply her handkerchief to her eyes and weep crocodile tears into it.

Taverner crossed the room and stood before me, looking down at the man on the bed without speaking. Then, raising his voice so that those on the other side of the room might hear, he said, "I have been called in by Lady Cullan, who wanted my advice as to your health, which has been causing her anxiety."

The Countess nudged her younger son to induce silence; she was quite satisfied as to her power over Taverner, but the Honourable John, having better brains, was not quite so sure of this man.

"I do not consider," continued Taverner, speaking slowly and weighing each word, "that it is wise for you to remain here, and I suggest that you should come to my nursing-home, and come now. In fact, I suggest that we should leave the house together."

I could see what Taverner's game was. Lady Cullan meant to have her eldest son certified, and his behaviour was sufficiently eccentric to make it very likely that she would succeed; if, however, he were at our nursing-home,

221

no other medical man would interfere; Taverner and I could use our own discretion whether we certified him or not, and we certainly should not do so unless it were in his interest as well as his family's. It was quite likely that Taverner would be able to put him on his feet and there would be no need to certify him at all; but that would not suit Lady Cullan's book, and if she had the least suspicion that we intended to do other than help her to lock the wretched man up for life, then we also should be discharged as 'not sufficiently careful'; some man with a licensed mental home would be called in, and Marius, Earl of Cullan, would speedily be under lock and key. It was for this reason that Taverner wanted to take him away then and there. But could he be induced to come? We could not constrain him unless we certified him. Would he, hounded as he had probably been all his life, trust anyone sufficiently to place himself in their hands? Would Taverner's personality sway him, or would he slip through our fingers into hands less clean? I felt as I used to feel in my student days when I saw dogs being taken up to the physiology laboratory.

But this man was as intuitive as a dog, and he sensed my feeling. He looked at me, and a faint smile curled his lips. Then he looked at Taverner.

"How do I know I can trust you?" he asked.

"You have got to trust somebody," said Taverner. "Look here, my dear fellow, you are in an uncommonly tight corner."

"I know it very well," said Lord Cullan, "but I am not sure I should not be in an even tighter corner if I trusted you."

It was a difficult situation. The poor chap was practically a prisoner in the hands of the most unpleasant and unscrupulous family, and unless we could protect him, he would be a prisoner in good earnest behind asylum bars. And whatever he was now, he would be most indubitably mad after a short course of asylum conditions. He was probably quite right when he said that he would die if deprived of his liberty, for he was of a type that easily become tubercular. Yet how were we to get him to trust us so that we could protect him?

Taverner joined me at the bedside, our two broad backs (we are both burly individuals) completely blocking out the rest of the party. He looked steadily at the man on the bed for a moment, then he said in a low voice, as if uttering a password:

"I am a friend of your people."

The dark eyes took on again their curious filmy look.

"What are my people like?"

"They are very beautiful," replied Taverner.

A snigger from the other end of the room showed how the rest of the family summed up the situation, but to my mind came the words of a seer—"How beautiful are they— the Lordly Ones, in the hills, in the hollow hills—"

"How do you know about my people?" said the man on the bed.

"Should I not know my own kind?" said Taverner.

I looked at him in amazement. I knew he never lied to a patient, yet what had he—cultured, urbane, eminent—in common with the wretched man lying on the bed, an outcast, for all his rank? And then I thought of the solitariness and secrecy of Taverner's soul; none knew him, not even I who worked with him day and night; and I remembered also the sympathy he had with the abnormal, the sub-human, and the pariah. Whatever mask he might elect to wear before his fellow men, there was some trait in Taverner's nature that gave him the right of way across the threshold into that strange hinterland of existence where dwell the lunatic and the genius; the former in its slums, and the latter in its palaces.

Taverner raised his voice. "I have been called in," he said, "by Lady Cullan, who desired my advice as to your health, which had been causing her anxiety. I am of the opinion that you are of an unusual heredity, and this has

223

made it difficult for you to adapt yourself to human society." (I saw that Taverner was picking his words carefully, and that they meant one thing to the man on the bed, and another to the Countess and her other son.)

"I am also of the opinion," Taverner went on, "that I could help you to make that adaptation because I understand your—heredity."

"In what way does his heredity differ from mine?" demanded the Honourable John, looking puzzled and suspicious.

"In every way," said Taverner. A peal of elfin laughter from the bed showed that at least one person knew what Taverner meant.

Taverner turned his back on the others and spoke to the man on the bed. "Will you come with me?" he said.

"Certainly," replied Lord Cullan, "but I should like to put some clothes on first."

At which hint we withdrew.

We seated ourselves in the broad window-seat of the oriel at the end of the passage, whence we could watch the door of Lord Cullan's room and so prevent our patient from giving us the slip. My medical training would have told me not to leave him alone at all, but apparently Taverner was quite certain he would not cut his throat and the rest of the family did not care if he did.

We had hardly seated ourselves before the Honourable John returned again to the question of the certification of his brother.

"I wish you would let us have that certificate now, Doctor," he said. "There are a number of matters in connection with the estate that urgently need attention."

Taverner shook his head. "Things cannot be done in this hasty fashion," he replied. "I must have your brother under my observation for a time before I can say whether he should be certified or not."

The three of them gazed at him, speechless with horror. This was an unexpected turn for affairs to take. The certi-

224

fication of a well-to-do eccentric is painfully easy if he remains in the bosom of his family, but it would be impossible to snaffle Marius out from under Taverner's nose if he once went to the nursing-home; he might remain there indefinitely, still retaining control of his affairs, effectually preventing his family from laying their hands on the cash, and he even might—awful thought—recover!

The Honourable John's mind worked more quickly than his mother's. She still seemed to have some vague idea that Taverner was safely in love with her; he saw plainly that they had been 'had,' and that Taverner not only had no intention of being their tool, but was prepared to stand by the unfortunate wretch against whom they were scheming, and see fair play. He lost no time in acting on his convictions.

"Well, Doctor," he said with the bullying insolence that lies so near the polished surface of men of this type, "we have heard your opinion, and we don't think very much of it, and should certainly not be guided by it. I told you all along, Mother, that we ought to have a first-class opinion on Marius and not depend on these local practitioners. We will not detain you any longer, Doctor," and he rose to show that the interview was at an end.

But Taverner sat like a hen, smiling sweetly.

"I have not expressed any opinion about yourself, Mr. Ingles, which is the only one you are entitled to ask me for; though if I had, I could quite understand your showing me the door in this somewhat brusque fashion. It is Lord Cullan who has done me the honour to place himself in my hands, and it is from him, and from no one else, that I shall take my dismissal, whether as his medical adviser or as a visitor to his house."

During the altercation the bedroom door had opened and Lord Cullan came up behind us, moving silently over the thick carpet. He had brushed his rough dark hair straight back from his forehead, revealing the fact that it grew in a peak, and this made him look even more elfin than the tangled black mat had done. Taverner's strictures on his family were evidently much to his taste, and his wide mouth, with its strangely unhuman thin red lips, was curled up on one side and down the other in a smile of puckish merriment. Lob-lie-by-the-fire, I christened him then, and the name has stuck to him ever since in that queer friendship into which we ultimately drifted.

He came up between Taverner and myself as we stood there, and threw his arms across our shoulders in a strange, un-English gesture expressive of affection. It seemed rather as if he took us under his protection than placed himself under ours, and it was in that light that our relationship has always stood, so defenceless on the physical plane, so potent in the realms of the Unseen, did Marius, Earl of Cullan, always show himself to be.

"Come!" he cried. "Let us get out of this house of evil; it is full of cruelty. It is a prison. These people are not real; they are unclean masks; there is nothing behind them. When the wind blows through them it sounds like words, but they cannot speak real words, for they are unensouled. Come, let us go away and forget them, for they are only bad dreams. But you" (touching Taverner) "have a soul; and he" (his hand fell upon my shoulder) "has also got a soul, though he doesn't know it. But I will give his soul to him, and make him know that it is his own, and then he will live, even as you and I live. Come, let us go! Let us go!"

Away he went down the long passage, swinging us with him by the compulsion of his magnetism, chanting "Unclean, unclean!" in that high, thrilling voice of his that seemed to curse the house as he went through it.

226

III

When we got him into the car, however, the reaction set in, and he was as unnerved as a child that suddenly finds itself alone on a stage before a great audience. Some unknown power had flowed through him a moment before, sweeping us all, friend and foe, along with irrestible force, but now he had lost his grip on it; it had left him, and he was defenceless, horrified at his own temerity, and watching us with furtive, anxious eyes to see what we were going to do to him now that he had betrayed himself by his outburst.

I thought that he was physically exhausted by the excitement through which he had passed, and therefore incapable of giving any trouble; but these queer cases in which Taverner specialised were very deceptive as to their physical condition; they had access to unsuspected reserves of strength which enabled them to rise as if from the dead. I am afraid that I was not watching our patient as closely as I should have been, for as the car slowed down to negotiate the park gates, he gave a sudden spring, leaped clean out of the car, and vanished into a thicket.

Taverner gave a long whistle.

"That is awkward," he said, "but not altogether to be wondered at. I thought he came a little too quietly to be altogether wholesome."

I rose up to jump out of the car and go in pursuit of our fugitive, but Taverner checked me.

"Let him go if he wants to," he said. "We have no power to coerce him, and are more likely to win his confidence by leaving him perfectly free to do as he pleases than by trying to persuade him to do what he has not got a mind to. It will do him no harm to sleep out in the open in this weather, and I have great faith in the power of the dinnergong. Cullan Court is the last place he is likely to make for, and they will be none the wiser as to his disappearance if we do not enlighten them.

"But here we are at Shottermill. Let us call in and see Parkes and hear what he has to say about the case. There are several points I want to clear up."

Dr. Parkes, the family physician of the Cullans, was one of the best of our local friends. He knew something of Taverner's speculations and was more than half inclined to sympathise, though fear for his practice kept him from identifying himself too openly with us.

He was an elderly bachelor, and welcomed us to his frugal lunch of cold mutton and beer. Taverner, who never wasted time in coming to the point if he had anything to say, opened the question of the mental condition of Lord Cullan. It was as we had suspected. For some time past Parkes had stood between him and certification, and was furious when he learnt that Lady Cullan had gone behind his back and called in Taverner; but he was also of the opinion that it would do our patient no harm to take to the heather. In fact, it was a thing that he frequently did, even in the winter, when family relations became especially difficult.

"You are the one man, Taverner," said our host, "who will be able to do anything in this matter. I have often thought over the case in the light of your theories, and they render explicable what would otherwise simply be a very odd coincidence, and science does not recognise coincidence, but only causation. I brought Marius into the world, and saw him through his measles and whooping-cough and all the rest of it, and I daresay I know him as well as any one does, which is not saying much, and the more I see of him, the less I understand him and the more he fascinates me. It is a queer thing—the fascination that lad has for fogies like myself; you would think we were poles asunder and would repel each other, but not a bit of it. To get friendly with Marius is like taking to drink— once you start, you can't stop."

This interested me, for I had an inkling of the same thing.

"The first time I saw Lord Cullan," I said, "I was very struck by his likeness to the old parson at Handley village. Is there any relationship between them?"

"Ah," said the doctor, "there you have put your finger upon a very curious thing. There is absolutely no connection between the two families save that the Cullans are the patrons of the living and inducted the old man into it, and I expect both parties heartily wish they hadn't. Mr. Hewins hates Marius like poison and made a great scandal once by refusing him the Sacrament; but what the relationship between them may be on what Taverner would call the Inner Planes—well, I might hazard a guess. Is there such a thing as being the spiritual grandfather of a person?"

"Generalisations are untrustworthy," said Taverner. "Give me some facts and I will be able to tell you more."

"Facts?" said Parkes, "there aren't any, save that the lad grows more like a caricature of Hewins year by year, and those who know the old story remark on it, yes, and make use of it, too. Now there is a farmer over at Kettlebury who won't turn the first furrow of a ploughing unless Marius leads the team—"

"Wait a bit," said Taverner. "Begin at the beginning, and tell us the old story."

"The old story," replied Parkes, "has nothing whatever to do with the matter, but here it is, for what it is worth.

"Hewins' wife was a daughter of one of the broom squires. I suppose you know who they are? Men, often of gypsy extraction, who have carved a holding out of the moor and hold it by squatter's right. It is a terribly hard and wild life, and the men are as hard and wild as the moor; as for the women, the less said about them the better.

"Well, Hewins married this girl for some reason best known to himself, and a more incongruous pair it would have been hard to find—her great-grandmother, by the way, was one of the last women to be put on trial for witchcraft in England—and they had a daughter called

229

Mary, who took after her mother and belonged to the heather rather than the glebe.

"Now this unfortunate girl, as ill luck would have it, fell in love with the late Lord Cullan, and he with her. It was all done quite openly, and everyone thought that the engagement would be announced, but apparently family pressure was brought to bear, and the next thing we knew was that he jilted little Mary of the vicarage and was married to the present Lady Cullan, Marius's mother. The disappointment proved too much for Mary, and she went out of her head, had to be removed to an asylum, and died there within the year, and her ravings, well, it didn't do for any one to hear them. If she had lived in her great-grandmother's time, she would probably have stood her trial for witchcraft too.

"Of course the whole incident made an unpleasant impression, and is still remembered among the country people hereabouts, though the Cullans' own set have forgotten it, if they ever knew it. One baby is very much like another, and Marius attracted no attention in his infancy, save for his peculiar name, which his father insisted on giving him, and for no reason assigned; but as he got big enough to show his colouring, it was remarked that although both the old earl and Lady Cullan were blondes, Marius was as black as a little tinker. He looked most odd and out of place in the nursery at Cullan Court, but you could have seen a dozen of him sprawling outside the broom squires' cottages; and as he got older, that was where he liked to go, and as a matter of fact, that is where he has probably gone at the moment.

"He never has anything to do with his own class, but he comes and goes about these moor holdings, goes into the kitchens and has a meal or a drink of milk, or sits by the fire for hours together on stormy days; doesn't tip the people, as you would expect, just asks for what he wants, has it, and goes, and they understand his ways; in return he seems to act as a kind of mascot at harvest and ploughing-time. From farms miles away he is invited to cut the first swathe at haying or walk in the furrow at seeding.

"You can form you own theories. I say nothing, save that year by year he gets more like old Hewins, and Hewins won't give him the Sacrament."

"I thought something of that kind must have been at the back of things," said Taverner.

"What do you propose to do with him, supposing he could be persuaded to let you treat him? Do you think it would be possible to get him normal?" Parkes enquired.

"What do you mean by normal?" countered Taverner. "Do you mean 'average' or 'harmonious'?"

But before the discussion could be developed further, a patient called and we took our leave.

"I am very much afraid," said I, "that they will succeed in locking that poor chap up after all if he wanders about the countryside, consorts with gypsies, and bewitches crops. Don't you think we ought to try and get hold of him?"

"I do," said Taverner, "but I shall use my own methods, and they will *not* consist of a glorified rat-hunt."

"There is a queer sort of bond," I said, "between Marius and us. Did you notice it?"

"Ah," said Taverner, "you felt a bond, did you? Now that greatly simplifies matters. You evidently have some sort of affinity with these children of Pan. You remember Diana, and the way she took to you?"*

I felt my ears get hot; I had no particular wish to be reminded of that incident.

"No," said Taverner, perceiving my feeling, "that had to be broken up because it would not have worked. Diana would have taken the whole of you and only satisfied a part if you had married her; but Marius, if you make friends with him, will deal with that level of your nature which belongs to his own kingdom and leave the rest free.

*See "A Daughter of Pan" (p. 109).

It seldom works for people of different rays and planes of development to marry each other under our existing marriage laws, but it is an excellent thing to have a diversity of friends because they develop aspects of one's nature that lie dormant, thereby rendering it incomplete."

IV

We had not long to wait for the raising of the curtain on the third act. That very evening, as I came out of the gate by the pillar-box, I saw the figure of a man standing on the edge of the moor, silhouetted against the sunset glow. I knew I could not be mistaken in the poise of that figure, although I could not see the face. Remembering Taverner's advice, I did not seek to approach him, but stood motionless by the gate, watching.

He had evidently been waiting for me, for when he heard the click of the latch, he turned and advanced a few yards.

"Do you expect me to come onto the cultivated ground to meet you, or will you come onto virginal soil to meet me?" he called across the intervening space.

"I will come onto the moor to meet you," I answered, and stepped off the paved road onto the sandy waste.

"What is your name?" he cried as I approached him.

"Rhodes," I answered, "Eric Rhodes."

"Ha," said he, "I shall call you Giles!"

He raised his hand to the branch of a birch-tree that hung just over our heads, and giving it a shake, brought down a shower of drops, for a storm had just passed.

"In my own name," he cried, "I baptise thee Giles."

(When I asked Taverner about this incident later, he said that it was the work of the witch-grandmother, but gave no further explanation.)

"Well?" said the Earl of Cullan, thrusting his hands into

232

the pockets of his disreputable tweeds and cocking his head on one side, "What do you people want with me? I am not quite so mad as I look, you know; I could behave decently if it did not bore me so much. But I have been fool enough to put myself on the wrong side of the lunacy laws, and I am, as you say, in a tight corner. Would you say a man was mad because he would not realise his capital in order to pay his brother's debts, with the certain knowledge that the payment of the said debts will be used as a means of obtaining further credit?"

"I shouldn't, personally," I replied. "But if a man combines any unusual form of behaviour with a tight hand on the family finances, it is quite likely that someone will be found, sooner or later, who can be induced to say so."

" 'If at first you don't succeed, try, try again,' seems to be my mother's motto," said Lord Cullan. "Now supposing I were to deposit my suitcase at your nursing-home—not that I need clean collars or any such frivolities, but just for the look of the thing—would you give me your word of honour that I should be treated as a visitor and not as a patient?"

"You must ask Dr. Taverner that," said I. "But if you trust him, I am sure you will not regret it."

Lord Cullan considered this for a moment, then nodded and returned with me to the nursing-home.

"Of course I gave him the promise he required," said Taverner when he told me of the subsequent interview. "I promised not to treat him, and neither will I, nor must you. Instead, I have given him a patient to handle on his own account."

"That patient being—?" said I.

"Yourself," said Taverner.

I gave a shout of laughter. "You're a downy bird!" I exclaimed.

"I really think I am," said Taverner, with a smile that was a little broader than the occasion seemed to warrant. "And I also think that I am not the only bird in the wood;

233

there are two others, and I shall kill them both with the same stone."

Marius evidently took his duties as my keeper perfectly seriously, and I, as Taverner wished, humoured him to the top of his bent. It was Taverner's custom, when he had a critical case, to devote himself to it for a few days and leave me to carry on the routine of the nursing-home, but in this case, he himself carried on the routine, and left me to deal with Marius.

Presently, however, I began to have a suspicion that Marius was dealing with me. His quick wits and shrewd, subtle brain made him the dominant member of the pair, and I soon realised that he, by means of pure intuition, was a better psychologist than I was or could ever hope to be, with all my training. Gradually he began to join the party in the office, which was against all professional etiquette, and most indiscreet in my opinion. I must confess to a twinge or two of jealousy at first as I heard Taverner asking his counsel and taking his advice with regard to certain cases that had puzzled us. Marius was far nearer to Taverner intellectually than I was. They both came from the same spiritual place in the hinter land of the subconscious, but in the one the scientist, and in the other, the artist, predominated. Taverner had saved his soul by masking it, whereas Marius had very nearly lost his by exposing it to vulgar eyes. As I listened to the talk round the consulting-room fire as the autumn evenings closed in, I often used to wonder how many of their spiritual kin were at that moment languishing in jails and madhouses, and why it was that civilisation must needs break such men as Marius on its wheel. I also realised why it is that the occultist works hidden under the protection of a fraternity sworn to secrecy, presenting to the world a mask such as Taverner wore, and hiding his real life from all save his brethern. Marius was a weaker man than Taverner, and had gone to the wall; whereas my chief, protected by the Order to which he belonged, handling by means of ritual the forces that ripped through Marius and tore him to bits, grew strong on that which consumed the other.

Taverner often threw us together in those days of early autumn that were gradually shortening into winter. Marius had a lot of estate business to transact, and it was my task to assist him. In money matters he was a child, and the moment he dealt with a tradesman was right royally swindled; but fortunately for him, the Cullan property was almost wholly in land, and for this he had a perfect genius, and for him land yielded in a peculiar way. The tenants regarded him with a superstitious veneration, and were, in my opinion, more than half-scared of him. They were, at any rate, very careful not to cross him, and to my certain knowledge he cast spells upon the fields, the farmer looking on with a sheepish grin, ashamed to admit his superstition, but desperately keen for the magic to be performed.

It could not go on forever, though, and the day came when I had to ask Taverner for a few days off in order to attend a medical conference in London. I got them readily enough—Marius, to my relief, agreeing to my departure without any fuss—and away I went, back to the haunts of men. This was the first time I had been at a gathering of my own kind since I had joined Taverner, and I was looking forward to it keenly. Here, I felt, my foot would be on my native heath; with Taverner I always felt somewhat a fish out of water.

But, as the different papers were read, and the discussions carried on, I found a peculiar sensation stealing over me. When I was with Taverner, my mind seemed to move slowly and clumsily by comparison; but by comparison with these men, my mind moved with a lightning speed and lucidity. As each fresh set of phenomena was described, I seemed to penetrate into the hidden life that actuated it; I did not see, as Marius saw, with clairvoyant light, but I knew things with an unerring intuition which I could not even explain to myself.

235

Still less could I explain it to others. And after one attempt to take part in the discussion, in which, it is true, I carried all before me, I withdrew into a silence which I allowed no probings to dispel. Over my soul there came a sense of utter solitude as I moved among these, my professional brethren; I felt as if I were looking in at a window rather than sharing in the conference. Until I returned to my old haunts I had not realised how far I had come along the path that Taverner trod; living always in his atmosphere, hearing his viewpoint, my soul had become tuned to the key-note of his, and I was set apart from my fellows. I knew I could enter into no relationship outside the strange, unorganised brotherhood of those who follow the Secret Path, and yet I was not of these either; an invisible barrier shut me off from them also and I could not enter into their life.

The conference terminated in a dinner, and I set out for this function in great turmoil of mind. More and more was borne upon me the fact of my isolation from those I had always regarded as my herd and looked to for support; more and more was borne upon me the need to push aside the veil behind which I had been vouchsafed many a momentary glimpse. The fact that I was Taverner's daily companion did not give me the right to pass behind the veil, however. I had, as it were, to enter the house of my soul and walk out through the back door. I cannot describe it better than that—the curious inturning which I felt I had to perform.

I had always feared that the inner depths of my soul were full of Freudian complexes and the things that wreck careers, and it was this idea that constituted a barrier; but now I realised what Marius had done for me during the weeks of constant companionship with his strange mind— the absolute naturalness of his outlook and the entire absence of any of the conventional social doctrines had gradually changed my sense of values. Like a silversmith, I did not look only at the elaborate workmanship of an object, but weighed the actual metal it contained; consequently there were some things I had valued highly which I no longer feared to lose.

And as I realised that I no longer valued the things that most men value, I suddenly felt that I dared reach out towards the things of the Unseen which I had long secretly coveted in spite of all my denials but had never dared to touch lest I should wreck my career by so doing. Oblivious to the crowded room and the prosing of the chairman, lost in a brown study, I pondered these things. I looked my life squarely in the face, and when I had finished, all the values were reassessed; I had indeed entered the house of life and passed through all the chambers.

And then, spontaneously and without effort, I opened the back door to my soul and stepped out into the wide and starry astral night. I saw infinite space crossed and recrossed by great Rays and sensed the passage of innumerable Presences. Then one of the rays fell across me and I felt as if something in my innermost substance caught Fire and shone.

The fit of abstraction passed and I became aware of my surroundings once more. The same speaker was prosing, no one had noticed my inattention. Time and space play no part in psychic experiences.

To my relief the dinner was nearing its end, and I escaped from the stewing atmosphere, heavy with reek of food and cigars, into the garish London night. There was no place here, however, where I could be alone with my thoughts, for humanity crowded about me. I had to have space and darkness for my soul to breathe in. Late as it was, I gathered up my belongings, got out the car, and set out down the Portsmouth road on the long road to Hindhead.

It was a road of many memories for me. Those who have read these chronicles know how often Taverner and I had raced up and down it on one or another of the adventures into which I had been led by my association with that strange and potent personality. It is true that I knew very little more about Taverner than I did at the beginning, but, ye gods, how much more I knew about myself! Supposing, I thought, Taverner and I for any reason were to part company, how would I manage to return to the world of men and find my place therein? Would I not be as alien as Marius? Those who enter the Unseen never really return, and unless I could find companionship in the place where I had gone, I should pass my life in spiritual solitude, with a terrible nostalgia of the soul for the bright places I had glimpsed.

Absorbed in my thoughts, I ran on past the turn that led to the nursing-home, and it was not until the engine cried out for a change of gear that I realised that I was climbing the heights of Hindhead. Below me lay the mist-filled hollow of the Punchbowl, looking like a lake in the moonlight, and above me the great Keltic Cross that gives rest to the souls of hanged men was silhouetted against the stars; all was very still and no air moved. In that enormous stillness of the open heaths, remote from all human life and thought, I felt the presence of an unseen existence above me, like walking through invisible water. The engine had come to a standstill on the gradient, and about me was absolute silence and darkness. Something was near. I knew it, and it was reaching out towards me; yet it could not touch me, for I had to take the first step. Should I do it? Should I dare to step outside the narrow limits of human experience into the expanse of wider consciousness that was all about me? Should I open that door which never can be closed again?

Above me on the hill the great granite cross cut the stars, a Keltic cross, with the circle of eternity superimposed on the outheld arms of renunciation. The mist had come up and blotted out the low-lying land over towards Frensham till I seemed to be alone on a crater of the moon. Cut off from all human influences, high up on the stark heights of the moors, I met my soul face to face while the unseen life that rose like a sea drew back as if to give me room for my decision.

And I hesitated, longing to plunge into that wonderful life, yet dreading it; when suddenly something gripped me by the heart and pulled me through. I cannot describe it better than that. I had passed an invisible barrier and was on the other side of it. Consciousness steadied again; the world was unchanged; there above my head still loomed the great cross, and yet in all things there was a profound difference; for to me, they had suddenly become alive. Not only were they alive, but I shared in their life, for I was one with them. And then I knew that, isolated though I must always be in the world of men, I had this infinite companionship all about me. I was no longer alone; for, like Taverner, Marius, and many others, I had passed over into the Unseen.

ABOUT THE AUTHOR

Dion Fortune is the pen name of Violet Firth, one of the most mysterious and significant figures of the British esoteric tradition of the early twentieth century. Born in Llandudno, Wales, in 1890, she exhibited strong psychic tendencies even as a child. She decided at a very early age to pursue a career in nursing, which led her quickly to an interest in human psychology. She became an early Freudian, but soon saw the limitations of psychoanalysis and pursued the deeper implications of human psychology in occult and magical traditions.

Raised on Christian Science, she gravitated first toward Theosophy and then to the Order of the Golden Dawn, where she became an initiate and received the hieratic name of Deo Non Fortuna, which eventually became her pen name, Dion Fortune. In 1922, she formed her own esoteric society, The Society of the Inner Light.

Dion Fortune's great legacy is her writings, both fiction and nonfiction. In nonfiction, her books *Psychic Self-Defence*, *The Mystical Qabalah*, *Through the Gates of Death*, and *Esoteric Philosophy of Love and Marriage* still stand, fifty years later, as the premier statements on their respective subjects. But it is in her fiction that she made her greatest contribution, probing depths of the human mind and character that conventional psychology still has not discovered—or understood.

The Secrets of Dr. Taverner is probably the most famous of her fiction. It is drawn from her own experiences in abnormal psychology, and the stories possess the immediacy and vitality that can come only from first-hand knowledge. It is said that Taverner is based on an initiate named Dr. Moriarity, with whom Dion Fortune worked.

She was married to, and divorced from, T. Penry Evans, M.D. She died in London in January, 1946. The Society of the Inner Light, however, is still in operation in England, and her books continue to be printed and reprinted.